# THE LIVELIHOOD OF KIN

# THE LIVELIHOOD OF KIN

BY RHODA HALPERIN

*Making Ends Meet "The Kentucky Way"*

 University of Texas Press, Austin

First Edition, 1990

⊗ The paper used in this publication meets the minimum
requirements of American National Standard for Information
Sciences—Permanence of Paper for Printed Library Materials,
ANSI Z39.48-1984.

**Library of Congress Cataloging-in-Publication Data**
Halperin, Rhoda H.
　　The livelihood of kin : making ends meet "the Kentucky
way" / by Rhoda H. Halperin.—1st ed.
　　　p.　　cm.
　　Includes bibliographical references and index.
　　ISBN 0-292-74669-5 (alk. paper).—ISBN 0-292-74670-9
(pbk. : alk. paper)
　　1. Kinship—Kentucky.　2. Economic anthropology—
Kentucky.　3. Biculturalism—Kentucky.　4. Kentucky—
Economic conditions.　5. Kentucky—Social life and
customs.　I. Title.
GN560.U6H35　1990
306.83—dc20
　　　　　　　　　　　　　　　　　　　90-37186
　　　　　　　　　　　　　　　　　　　CIP

This book is dedicated to Deb, without whom this study would not have even begun

# Contents

# Preface

*"Hey, India, where does your daddy live?"*
*She sat up, and for a moment I was afraid she would run away too.*
*"Ohio," she said. "He's way off in Cincinnati, Ohio."*

Willis (1975:48)

To the energy, resourcefulness, ingenuity, and resiliency of rural people all over the world.

To the students who listen silently in urban classrooms—who feel uncomfortable, as one does in an unfamiliar culture—but who pretend not to let on, unless the professor indicates that it is acceptable to talk about going home to help kin in the country.

To the young patients and their families who suffer in the transitions—the transitions to adulthood and the transitions to life in the city.

This book is about the relationships between family and economy in an unstudied part of rural Appalachian America. That the field research happened to take place in rural Kentucky is secondary to the fact that the issues concerning basic strategies for livelihood are widespread in the rural United States, as well as other parts of the world where similar kinds of economic changes associated with industrialization, deindustrialization, urbanization, and resistance to urbanization are taking place. This study began to take shape several years ago when in my office a very bright student, one day early in her graduate career, suddenly adopted the tone of a confessional and announced that she spoke two dialects of English: "country" and "city." She paused, and with some tension in her voice, told me how much she feared lapsing into "country" English while concentrating so hard to speak "city" (or standard) English to her university professors. After I assured her that I would think no less of her if she used either dialect, she volunteered that she used "country" English at her parents' home in a rural area of northeastern Kentucky. There she experienced another sort of anxiety. If she slipped into "city" English, her Mom and Dad would consider her snobbish and uppity. I was certainly well aware of the abilities of speakers of Black English to switch back and forth from one dialect of English to another. Discussions with African American students revealed that switching dialects also meant switching cultures. As a relative newcomer to the Appalachian region, however, I had not considered the issue of "biculturality" for Appalachian students. Before having the conflicts between the uses of the two dialects of English pointed out to me, I had not, in all honesty, given the problem a great deal of thought. In fact, I had been deceived by this student's virtually perfect standard English. That she was indeed a member of the "Invisible Minority" (Philliber and McCoy 1981), a term used to describe urban Appalachian migrants, had also not been apparent to me. The implications that she too was living in two cultures, which at that point I could only label urban and rural, were becoming more and more profound. I realize now that whenever I struggle to read passages of another dialect of English aloud in class, my students laugh at my awkwardness—but they understand.

Several years after the conversation with the student about switching between country and city English, following a lecture and discussion for beginning anthropology students about the difficulties experienced by rural Brazilians when their villages undergo rapid industrialization, another student, this time an undergraduate, accosted me after class to tell me about her friend who lived in Lower Price Hill, an urban Appalachian community in Cincinnati. She said that our discussion reminded her of the stories her close childhood friend had related about growing up with an alcoholic father and a mother who was exhausted by shouldering single-handedly the responsibilities of work and family. I nodded knowingly and said something abstract and professorial about how important a cross-cultural comparative perspective could be for understanding rural-to-urban migration patterns and processes of cultural change. As I walked back from class to my office, the expression on that student's face and the emotion in her voice lingered in my mind.

Several weeks later, the same student spoke to me again. This time the class had been reading about the United States—people from the rural South, and the consequences of their moves to northern American cities. We had been discussing different kinds of economic adaptations, rural and urban, and their implications for understanding problems of gender, race, and class. Some uneasiness had come over the class as we compared people of different races in similar environments—for example, poor urban people, both black and white. A few students squirmed in their seats; others looked anxiously at the clock. As the hour came to a close, notebooks slammed shut and backpacks came out from under the seats. When the class was over, the same young woman walked with me back to the Anthropology Department. She shifted from one foot to the other as I fumbled with my key to unlock the door. As she sat down she began to speak. Her upper lip quivered, and her nervousness caused me to struggle to remain calm.

"Remember a few weeks ago when I was telling you about my friend from Price Hill?"

"Yes," I replied somewhat tentatively, at that instant not quite remembering the details.

"The friend was me."

For purposes of preserving the anonymity of the individuals and families who participated in this research, I have taken some small liberties with names and with the details of some events. The names of people and places are used consistently, however, so that particular individuals and families can be followed.

In compliance with the wishes of the people in rural Kentucky who gave so generously of their time and emotions, the specific counties in this study have been carefully disguised. It was a struggle to make this judgment, since, for comparative purposes, identifying specific counties would be important. Ultimately, the decision to change the names of people and places and to eliminate maps of the region rested upon our respect for people's privacy. Given that not just one, but several, informal economies are at work in this part of Appalachia, the decision seems to make sense.

Many people contributed their time and their energy to this study: students, colleagues, and most important, those who shared their everyday lives and livelihood. Theresa and Brian Hageman, Heidi Lippmeier, and Wendy Cameron helped collect data. Sara Sturdevant has been with this project as fieldworker and data analyst from its inception to its conclusion—first as an undergraduate and then as a graduate student. She is the co-author of three chapters and has made major contributions to the entire book. She grew up as an anthropologist with this project.

Special thanks go to the Research Council of the University of Cincinnati for providing some of the initial funding for this project. I also am thankful to the University of Cincinnati's Center for the Study of Work and Family, especially Paula Dubeck, the director, for providing additional funding for data collection and analysis. Many colleagues gave their time to read this manuscript and to discuss ideas, however tangentially related. Patricia Beaver pointed me to the work of Guerney Norman. Ken Kensinger, Rubie Watson, Sally Merry, and Susan Keefe provided extremely helpful suggestions at several stages. Marcia Slomowitz, Kathryn Borman, Nola Hadley, and Chris Anderson also commented on the work. Graduate students Dari Malloy and Kathy Berger helped with the bibliography as did Sandi Cannell of the Department of Anthropology at Cincinnati. Maria Swarts gave invaluable editorial assistance.

To the program in Anthropology and Archaeology at MIT I owe special thanks for the quiet office space and the exceptional support of the faculty and staff during my sabbatical year there. Jim Howe, Jean Jackson, Martin Diskin, Heather Lechtman, Arthur Steinberg, Alison Salisbury, and Virginia Moser all went out of their way to provide an ideal working environment. Jonathan Wylie provided many useful thoughts and references on comparative European ethnography. To the people at the University of Texas Press I owe special thanks. Theresa May's enthusiasm for the project provided a timetable for its completion, and Barbara Spielman and Barbara Cummings gave excellent editorial assistance.

# THE LIVELIHOOD OF KIN

# ONE

# *Introduction*

*Mary Lou Skaggs runs errands for her husband. She hauls lumber, delivers bookshelves, even makes a special trip to town just to exchange flathead screws. Mack will occasionally go out to measure people's kitchens for the cabinets and countertops he makes, but he gets uncomfortable if he has to be away long. And the highway makes him nervous. Increasingly, he stays at home, working in his shop in the basement. They live on a main road between two small Kentucky towns. . . . Mary Lou feels that Mack never charges enough for his work, but she has always helped out—keeping the books, canning and sewing, as well as periodically working for H & R Block—and they have managed to send their youngest child to college.*

*Mason (1982:17)*

*The ministry is not a full-time calling, Georgeann discovered. The pay is too low. While Shelby attended seminary, he also went to night school to learn a trade, and Georgeann supported him working at Kroger's—the same one her husband had robbed. Georgeann had wanted to go to college, but they were never able to afford for her to go.*

*Now they have two children, Tamara and Jason. During the week, Shelby is an electrician, working out of his van.*

*Mason (1982:132)*

*The Livelihood of Kin* is an anthropological treatment of the complex relationships between economy and kinship—what people in northeastern Kentucky call "the Kentucky way." The Kentucky way is making a living in the self-reliant, steadfast Kentucky style. From the outset the research problems and research strategies, the energy and the stamina so necessary to carry out this work, were encouraged and nurtured in true Kentucky fashion by many rural people for whom it was important that a way of life that is deeply rooted, lasting, and resilient be set on paper. I should emphasize that the economic strategies encompassed by the folk expression "the Kentucky way" are not unique to Kentucky or to Appalachia; these economic strategies operate in many rural parts of the world and encompass the core principles and guidelines for making a living.

In fact, throughout the course of the fieldwork, much of what I heard and saw expressed as the Kentucky way seemed familiar, as though I had experienced these things before. The quality of people's lives; the nature of their long-lasting and highly reliable relationships with other people, especially relatives, but also neighbors and friends; the fact that people could be counted upon to "be there" (to help out, to provide food and transportation) when they were most needed, reminded me of time I had spent in Caribbean villages and in small towns and villages in Mexico. I realized that what people called the Kentucky way is generalizable, if not universal; it has many manifestations and variations all over the rural landscape. The Kentucky way is, quite literally, a way of life based on ties to land and family that confers dignity and self-esteem upon rural working-class people.

The people described in this book are difficult to classify. They do not fit into conventional pigeonholes, and whatever labels one tries to use somehow seem inappropriate. People live in rural areas, and many work or have worked in cities, but the terms "peasants" and "workers" somehow do not capture the essence of their livelihood patterns. By the same token, people plant gardens and cash crops, but they are not farmers in the conventional sense of that term; neither are they simply wage workers. Their work tasks are numerous and change weekly, seasonally, and generationally; work occupies people throughout the life course: from childhood, through adulthood, and into old age. What remain stable are people's ties to land and their strong commitments to family—understood here as a large network of kinspeople spread throughout a 10-county region. The commitments are played out regularly—but in highly complicated ways—in the course of carrying out the ordinary tasks of livelihood. Because they do not fit any of the conventional categories, they have received little attention from social scientists.[1]

This study is an economic ethnography: economic in its focus on livelihood, ethnographic in its insistence upon treating the problem of livelihood in the varied and changing contexts within which people work to make ends meet. As for its genre, this book falls under the rubric of economic anthropology, which can be understood as the anthropology of livelihood—of the ordinary, the mundane, and the practical—the everyday stuff of material life and the provisioning processes that furnish material means.[2] That most of the people described in this book live in rural areas that are very close to cities and that some currently live, however transiently or temporarily, in cities connects them with rural working people in similar circumstances throughout the world. The ways in which people generate the basic material means necessary for livelihood occupy the attention of all chapters. But just as truth is often stranger than fiction, so is the ordinary often more intricate and more puzzling—more difficult to fathom—than the exotic and the bizarre. Why do family-oriented multiple livelihood strategies persist? What are the forces and processes that enable people to maintain the Kentucky way in rural places and in places with solid rural connections? This way of life and livelihood is not possible under circumstances in which urbanization renders people isolated from family land and in which family bonds stretch to the breaking point.

This study focuses on Appalachians as rural working-class people. It grew out of a series of anthropological field studies of ways of making a living—or multiple livelihood strategies—in a complex and rapidly changing part of the Appalachian region over a period of almost six years. The studies were based in three different parts of an area encompassing northeastern Kentucky and southern Ohio. The comparative perspective that anthropology brings to this analysis is critical. The concepts developed here should be useful not only in other parts of the United States but also globally in areas undergoing similar processes of rural to urban migration and rapid economic changes. What is unusual, although not unique, about the people who practice the Kentucky way is that they have managed to maintain traditional patterns of social and economic life—strong kin and community ties and family economies—outside of household and community contexts. They are not marginal. Indeed, they have resisted marginality by using both their social (family) and their economic (land) resources in innovative and flexible, but at the same time, traditional rural ways. They have managed to transform traditional patterns of livelihood in positive and culturally consistent ways.

Uniting this diverse area is the cultural term referred to as "the Kentucky way." The second chapter delineates the dimensions of this system of local, practical knowledge—its essential rural ("country") orientation and its pervasiveness in defining "the way we do things here." The manifestations of the Kentucky way are played out in all parts of the region in crosscutting patterns: homeplace ties, loyalty and generosity to kin, commitment to versatility, self-sufficiency, and self-reliance. The essence of the Kentucky way involves maintaining family ties even in the face of great geographical distances between related households and extraordinary work schedules. It is people's loyalty to and belief in the Kentucky way that provides them with a sense of autonomy and control over their lives and their livelihood, allowing people to resist dependency upon capitalism.

Chapter 2 also introduces two new and central concepts, that of the "shallow rural"—a term referring to the middle ground between country and city—and that of "multiple livelihood strategies." The concept of the shallow rural is designed to overcome the traditional and well-entrenched dichotomy between rural and urban. The shallow rural is a predominantly rural area that contains the most intricate mix of livelihood strategies because of its location in the middle ground between "country" and "city." Rural homesteads with subsistence gardens, factories employing primarily temporary wage laborers, and marketplaces ("flea markets"), organized hierarchically in the form of a rotating periodic marketplace system are all found there and used as elements of livelihood. The Kentucky way is accentuated in the shallow rural. The concept of multiple livelihood strategies is an attempt to overcome the conventional dichotomies: formal and informal and capitalist and non-capitalist economies. It is designed to describe modes of livelihood that are neither rural nor urban, capitalist nor precapitalist, but combinations of these. Both of these concepts are analytic tools for understanding a generalizable cultural response to a widespread contemporary situation—processes of industrialization and deindustrialization, urbanization and resistance to it.

The third chapter describes the field research for this book. It highlights the fact that the fieldworkers functioned as a team made up of undergraduates, graduate students, and university faculty and staff. The costs and benefits of conducting fieldwork in a regional setting (communities, marketplaces, factories, and an urban psychiatric unit) over a six-year period "at home," so to speak, are discussed in this chapter. The subtleties of cultural cues and dialectical differences, as well as the tensions between "country people" and "city people," are central themes in this chapter.

"Kinship," "residence," and "household" are concepts that have been used in problematical ways in the Appalachian literature. Chapter 4 includes a discussion of the limitations of the household as the primary unit of economic organization, emphasizing the trinity of family, land, and community and their economic and psychological significance. Noncapitalist economic patterns remain prominent.

Chapter 5 examines multiple livelihood strategies in the deep rural by portraying combinations of work on family-based subsistence farms, wage labor, and service jobs as experienced through the lives of two elderly women.

The intersection of economic and family life is portrayed in the residential context of a hamlet in the shallow rural. Multiple livelihood strategies carry over to the shallow rural, but change their form. Chapter 6 presents five families in this shallow rural hamlet whose kin networks extend throughout the 10-county region. People in these networks work in the agrarian, marketplace, and factory economies and coordinate their activities through informal systems of exchange. The hamlet provides a focus for understanding the strong agrarian base of regional family networks and the complexities of their multiple livelihood strategies.

The informal economy of the rotating periodic marketplace system is the subject of the next two chapters. These marketplaces are clearly outside the mainstream economy and are, in this sense, informal. Marketplaces operate with noncapitalist relations of production, but use the products of capitalist as well as noncapitalist forms of economic organization. They sell the seconds and rejects of large companies, and they also sell old things from the garages and attics of relatives and friends, from auctions and garage sales, and from the labor of family members in craft and food production. This study is not an ethnography of marketplaces, but rather a focused treatment of the structure and use of marketplaces in the context of the overall pattern of multiple livelihood strategies. Marketing is only one piece of the Kentucky way.

Another part of livelihood derives from wage labor. Chapter 9 uses a set of work histories to show how people use wage labor as a cash-generating strategy. When wage labor is part of the complex of multiple livelihood strategies, and when it operates in the context of the extended family network, people move in and out of factory jobs and maintain their abilities to control their working lives. It is when people become simultaneously wrenched from their kin networks and dependent upon cash for the totality of their livelihood that serious problems, both economic and psychological, arise for families. Chapter 10 describes some of the psychiatric problems that can arise for adolescent girls of rural Appalachian origin as they try to live simultaneously in urban and rural cultures without being able to commit themselves to either.

The concluding chapter deals with the boundaries of rural and urban, capitalist and precapitalist, formal and informal economies. Resistance to capitalism requires all of these in creative combinations.

The usual conceptual boundaries—especially the conventional dichotomies of rural versus urban, capitalist versus noncapitalist, market versus nonmarket, formal versus informal economy, to name a few— that anthropologists and others have drawn for purposes of examining workers, peasants, communities, regions—even economies—are, for the most part, held in abeyance in this book. The people in northeastern Kentucky are simultaneously migrants, small landholders, workers, craftspeople, and shrewd businesspeople. A sense of commercial savvy and entrepreneurship is, and has been, a part of Appalachian economic life for at least two centuries. To use the label capitalist, or even "penny capitalist," to describe the people or their economic activities, would be to oversimplify a complex set of intertwining relationships and processes that operate between local and national economies and among kin dispersed throughout a 10-county region. By the same token, people's economic activities should not be interpreted to be exclusively anticapitalist or noncapitalist. Rather, the economy that best characterizes the Kentucky way is a complex family-oriented economy. The word "complex" is important here because it indicates that the context within which people pursue their livelihood is a highly stratified, capitalistic, postindustrial state, and multinational system. The word "family" should be understood as an extended, three-generation family network whose members are dispersed throughout the region. The economy of the rural, working-class people who practice the Kentucky way is best characterized as familial because family imperatives dominate choices of work tasks; in many instances kin units are also units of production.

Units of description and analysis are also problematic. This is not a community study, yet there is ethnographic material about a community and about a settlement (hamlet) that is part of a community. The largest and primary geographical unit is a 10-county segment of the Appalachian region. Yet even a regional unit is, in some respects, too confining for purposes of understanding the persistence of the patterns of complex and multiple livelihood strategies: their agrarian base and their essential family orientation. The region is itself, then, an arbitrary unit. It is large enough to operate with, for purposes of setting some spatial boundaries, yet small enough for understanding the problem at hand. I should note also that the region itself does not fit the conventional stereotypes of Appalachia. It is not presently nor historically a coal-mining area. Neither is it mountainous. It is not isolated but is very much interconnected with a whole variety of different kinds of economic formations. The kin network is, in fact, the major instrument for making these connections. In other words, the region is somewhere in between the core and the periphery of economic life in the United States. There are probably many such in-between areas. At the same time, people are closely knit, and they can easily spot an outsider.

Roughly speaking, one may identify three economic sectors in the region. These sectors must be understood as combinations of capitalist and noncapitalist, formal and informal economies: (1) the agrarian sector of farms and gardens with both subsistence and cash-cropping components, (2) the wage labor sector that consists primarily, but not exclusively, of factory-based work, and (3) a system of rotating periodic marketplaces that is used by market sellers as a source of cash and by market buyers as a source of inexpensive necessities. Virtually no one works in any single sector on a full-time basis for a lifetime. Rather, all three sectors are used by people in some fashion as they pursue their livelihood as members of kin networks: nonresidential, regionally dispersed, and three-generation extended families. People work in cooperation with kin within the region. People obtain jobs in the region through kin networks. Some may venture outside the region, but most return home sooner or later. The kin groups are not confined to households or to communities. Segments of extended families live and work in various parts of the region. They almost never come together in one place, yet they maintain their economic ties to one another in intricate and often very subtle ways. People use cash generated by selling "old things" in marketplaces to support their farms. They maintain and strengthen kin ties by exchanging food, labor, tools, guns, and so forth. These exchanges may or may not take place in the marketplace. Again, all of these exchanges operate within a regional context.

The agrarian holdings in this region are and have always been small; they are oriented toward the maintenance of the kin network, both materially and psychologically. The agrarian units are themselves diverse, however. Some are small family farm enterprises with acres devoted to cash crops (primarily burley tobacco) and to feed for livestock. Truck farming and subsistence gardening are common. Average farm size in the region is 121 acres, and this is considered by most to be a large farm. (The mean is skewed by a few large farms; only 2 percent of the farms are over 500 acres.) Some other agrarian units are simply households located on small holdings with subsistence gardens; still others are combinations of farms, gardens, and workshops (welding, crafts, furniture, repairs, etc.). The agrarian holdings provide the baselines from which family members move back and forth from their wage labor jobs and from their buying and selling activities in the marketplaces. Some might categorize the economic activities described in this book, especially those in the marketplaces, as belonging to the informal sector— the hidden or the underground economy. Indeed, it is true that many of the transactions will never appear in any official records and certainly not in the systems of national accounts. Even the category "informal sector" is problematic because its boundaries in this regional system of multiple livelihood strategies cannot be drawn easily.

Given the inadequacy of conventional concepts, this book has had to move into unknown territory, terminologically as well as conceptually. The choice of terms and terminology is critical because it shapes our thinking. For example, even the seemingly simple term "job" is difficult to use in connection with the Kentucky way. This is true in part because people have many jobs in a lifetime. It is also true because so many time-consuming and viable work activities are never called jobs by anyone—neither by people actually doing the work nor by social scientists.

I have had to create some new, and resurrect some old, analytic concepts and methods for understanding livelihood processes in this region. The reader will have to pay close attention to the methods, the signals, and the signposts I have created in order to understand the basic framework I have established for understanding "the livelihood of kin." One method has been to examine the negative case—that is, what happens when kin networks and thus livelihood processes break down? The positive features of livelihood strategies are thrown into sharp relief by using this method. I have been fortunate to have access to psychiatric case histories of hospitalized Appalachian adolescents to be able to examine the relationships between livelihood processes, family structure, and psychiatric disorders.

We are accustomed to reading about the ways in which people cope with change, uncertainty, and poverty. There has been little discussion, however, of the costs—both economic and psychological, to individuals and to families—of coping with urban life or of maintaining kin networks when segments of the networks are both geographically distant and culturally at odds with other segments. When nuclear families move to cities without kin, they create conflict within the networks that cause the flexibility of multiple livelihood strategies to disappear. Individual women cannot cope with children and with full-time jobs. Adolescents cannot simultaneously cope with school obligations and cater to the needs of their younger siblings and their grandparents who reside in the country. For some adolescents the costs become unbearable, and they become hospitalized. This does not mean that all people, or even all adolescents, who move to the city become mentally ill. It does draw attention to what happens in the most extreme cases of maladaptation to urban life because the patient cases illustrate the difficulty of putting together a combination of viable livelihood strategies in the absence of kin networks in the city.

The concepts employed herein are analytic concepts, not folk concepts. They are designed to explain the behavior of "the folk," and they derive from folk concepts as I have filtered them through the lenses of the problem of livelihood. The concepts and their relationships to the "on the ground" (actual) behavior are not meant to be presented in an oversimplified or overly positivistic way. There are no absolute truths, no right or wrong interpretations of the data—only interpretations that are more or less supported by the evidence at hand. People who grew up in cities will read the evidence differently from people raised in the country. That is, different readers, young and old, rural and urban, will see different aspects of the data as important. Educators will read differently from health practitioners. For some these data will strike close to home. The data may even trigger a broad spectrum of raw emotions: warmth, nostalgia, sadness, anger. For others the people in this book will occupy the place of "the other," and distance from their lives and their livelihoods will be easy. Indeed, the process of sifting and sorting the ethnographic inputs—weighing the interpretations and reactions of an urban born and reared anthropologist against those of the rural people—has been a constant and difficult process.

TWO

# *An Overview*

*"Country" and "city" are very powerful words, and this is not surprising when we remember how much they seem to stand for in the experience of human communities. In English, "country" is both a nation and a part of a "land"; "the country" can be the whole society or its rural area. In the long history of human settlements, this connection between the land from which directly or indirectly we all get our living and the achievements of human society has been deeply known. . . .*

*On the actual settlements, which in the real history have been astonishingly varied, powerful feelings have gathered and have been generalized. On the country has gathered the idea of a natural way of life; of peace, innocence, and simple virtue. On the city has gathered the idea of an achieved centre: of learning, communication, light. Powerful hostile associations have also developed: on the city as a place of noise, worldliness and ambition; on the country as a place of backwardness, ignorance, limitation.*

*Williams (1973:1)*

## THE KENTUCKY WAY: AUTONOMY AND CONTROL OF LIVES AND LIVELIHOOD

The folk (working-class people) in northeastern Kentucky talk about the Kentucky way, sometimes with nostalgia, sometimes with regret, but always with affection and respect. The expression "the Kentucky way" is repeated often; it is familiar to all. It is the expression most commonly used by people to describe "the way we do things here." As such, the Kentucky way refers to a broad spectrum of practical skills and knowledge of local resources. It identifies people with one another. It is something about which there is often heightened consciousness, but it is at the same time extremely subtle, especially to the outsider.

"You must record 'the Kentucky way' before it disappears," said a young country woman. At first I was somewhat flattered by her willingness to give me such responsibility. I was also taken aback by the task that had just been assigned, namely that of salvaging something so essential to the culture before it changes or is eliminated. But what is "the Kentucky way"? Why is it so important, so precious, and so vulnerable? The Kentucky way provides the keystones and conceptual maps for making a living and for living itself.

The Kentucky way is primarily a system of local knowledge and practices that allows people to exercise control over their livelihood and that provides them with a sense of autonomy (Geertz 1983). Often people speak of the Kentucky way in a religious idiom, especially when they are talking about work. People say such things as "The idle body is a sin," or "I am working for the Lord," or "God sits above the government."

At its core the Kentucky way is about maintaining livelihood and maintaining rural culture. It includes commitments to kin, to hard work and self-sufficiency, to freedom and to the land, to generosity and reciprocity, and to certain kinds of practical knowledge. Economic knowledge itself is based on rural skills, but most important it involves knowing something about everything within the appropriate male and female domains, many of which are overlapping. On one level, local knowledge translates into being "a jack of all trades" and should be understood as a positive and self-conscious effort by people to maintain a general repertoire of skills. People resist becoming specialists who must rely on others to perform tasks for them. Self-sufficiency is extremely important to people in this region, for it is a strategy of self-reliance, a mark of one's versatility and flexibility and one's ingenuity and cleverness. In this region self-reliance does not serve to isolate people.[1] It is not individualistic or self-serving. Rather, it is a form of outreach to kin and to neighbors in the context of offering multiple goods and services in multiple arenas. The fact that people are so versatile creates great flexibility for livelihood strategies. Not only can people choose easily between various work tasks, they can switch from one task to another in accordance with the needs of family members and with the opportunities made available through kinship ties.

For both men and women, knowledge of the local ecology is essential for knowing when and how to hunt, fish, and gather. Hunting and fishing are not mere sport in this area; they provide essential protein. Knowledge of the land, its virtues, limitations, and seasonal patterns, are certainly important for all agricultural societies, but the Kentucky way reinforces the importance of agrarian skills in combination with the mechanical skills necessary for keeping machinery, vehicles, and households functioning. One man proudly told us how he could tune up his pick-up truck for a fraction of what it would cost him to take the truck to the local garage.

Being a good Kentucky woman (homemaker and worker in the widest sense of these terms) is an essential part of the Kentucky way. Women pass down knowledge of food production (gardening), processing (canning and freezing), and storage techniques from generation to generation. For women as well as for men, knowing how to be resourceful is regarded as the essence of the good person. Women also resist specialization but in ways that are both similar to and different from those of men. For both men and women, maintaining one's position in trade networks and social groups leads to knowledge about which marketplaces are best for selling or buying particular items. Men and women sell and trade different kinds of things, however, and they engage in different kinds of social groups. Social groups of women are often church based. Through these groups, women exchange food, provide help with children, and donate time for home health care on both a long-term and an emergency basis. Social groups of men are much smaller and more informal. It is not uncommon to see men gathered in groups of two or three on porches, in the aisles of marketplaces, or almost anywhere.

People see greater opportunities to use a variety of resources in the country. They see themselves as belonging to the country and as country people, even though they live, many of them, less than five miles from a city. In the context of understanding livelihood processes, "belonging to the country" involves the mastery of practical knowledge through apprenticeships and close intergenerational ties. Older Kentuckians lament the proliferation of young "shut-ins," a folk term for people who live in apartments, work at unskilled and low-paying wage labor jobs, and watch television and drink beer in their spare time. In analytical terms these are people who, by refusing to engage in learning the spectrum of practical skills, prevent the production and reproduction of local practical knowledge. From the point of view of older people in the region, these young adults are putting themselves in a very vulnerable position. That is, without practical local knowledge of agrarian skills, for example, people become completely dependent upon cash generated in the wage labor sector. When they are inevitably laid off, unless family members "help them out," they become dependent upon the welfare system, something that is an anathema to the Kentucky way because it flies in the face of self-sufficiency and local autonomy.

One aspect of mastering local knowledge requires knowing how to use the market (capitalist) economy without succumbing to it—that is, without becoming completely dependent upon cash. The distinction between a market system (abstract market economy) and a marketplace system (a set of locations in which goods are distributed) is important.

The term "market economy" refers to an institution that organizes transactions that are determined by a supply and demand price mechanism. The term "marketplace" refers to a physical location in which transactions of all sorts (market and nonmarket) can occur. The term "market economy" is used throughout to refer to the capitalist market system. The terms "marketplace" or "marketplace system" are used to refer to a location or set of locations. Under the rubric of "the Kentucky way," economic knowledge involves a complex set of economic activities that operate in intricate relationships to the market economy. In many instances, people engage simultaneously in parallel market and nonmarket activities.[2] For example, they may work in both the wage labor sector and in the agrarian subsistence sector. Or they may engage in activities that are completely outside the mainstream of the market economy, such as illegal gun sales. Many economic activities in the region are not market driven in the sense that they operate outside of the mainstream capitalist economy; at the same time these activities involve a creative use of the market economy. People use the products (often the rejects, seconds, etc.) of the market system as goods to sell in marketplaces. As far as it is possible, people avoid making purchases in the mainstream market economy. Therefore, the system of marketplaces figures prominently because its structure enables rural social organization to flourish, and it provides the context within which local knowledge can be reproduced in ways that are adaptive to the constantly changing regional and national economy.

One of the ways local knowledge is reproduced is through apprenticeships. For example, within the marketplace, children and adolescents work under the tutelage of older kin. Children survey other booths, which are sources of goods for resale as well as consumables, with an eye for price and to check on available bargains. They sell their own wares in the corner of an adult's booth. They help organize goods and watch over neighboring booths. Apprenticeships assure the continuity of skills from one generation to another.

By using the wage labor economy only in circumstances where immediate cash is required or in instances in which there are no other alternatives, some people resist contributing their labor to the market economy. In order to engage in this form of resistance to capitalism, people must have alternative sources of cash. Marketplaces provide one such alternative. In order to operate successfully in the marketplaces, however, one must "know people" and "know the ropes," two not unrelated aspects of success. Family and regional connections, many of which overlap, are essential.

Analytically speaking, the Kentucky way signifies certain kinds of ideal relations to the means of production, especially to land. Owning land, "private property," however small one's plot may be, operates as a buffer against dependency upon outsiders. There are certain conditions attached to owning land, however. Land sufficient for a large subsistence garden as well as for a plot on which a cash crop (usually tobacco) can be grown is most desirable, for example. One important aspect of self-sufficiency requires that agrarian units remain debt free. Ties to rural homeplaces can be understood in this context not only as sources of debt-free land but, more important, as reservoirs of local knowledge and the resources this knowledge provides.

The Kentucky way also indicates relationships to regional and state authorities. The Kentucky way is a form of identity, an attachment to rural as opposed to urban life-styles. Disdain for industrialism and for economic development (in the conventional sense of the term) is part of the Kentucky way. I remember being driven around the region one afternoon when my attention was directed to the posted signs that read "Let Toyota be your neighbor." "This is terrible," said one of the region's residents. "This is ruining our farms." Many people express a strong resentment of the defacement of the countryside by, in this case, foreign industrialists. One hears negative comments about the governor's lack of sensitivity to the needs of the people. In part, the negativism stems from the fact that people do not perceive jobs as providing a secure or sufficient livelihood. Combined here is disdain not only for industry but for those in power. "People are made into machines in those factories," one man told me. The Toyota plant, which opened within the last few years, did indeed encompass the entire horizon. I was urged to photograph one particular spot in which the plant spanned the horizon; a barn occupied the background, and a lone horse, the foreground. "See," one man said, "all the trees have been cut down; no berries and no rabbits could live there now."

Participating in the Kentucky way carries certain obligations as well as certain rights. Critical among the obligations are those to family members. Making a living must never interfere with these obligations. At least ideally, making ends meet should contribute to family well-being. If, for example, a young adult chooses to take a job that is located too far for kin to visit easily, he or she will be the object of criticism. Also, staying in school too long for the pursuit of advanced degrees can be negatively regarded. Questions from parents such as, "Haven't you been in school long enough? When are you going to get a *real* job?" are frequently heard.

Perhaps one of the best ways to understand the Kentucky way is as a form of what Daniela Weinberg has called the traditional ideology of "peasant wisdom": "the wisdom to remain free of outside control by owning and managing a variety of resources, and free of debt by running a self supporting household" (1975 : 196). The key component of peasant wisdom, Kentucky style, is control over one's day-to-day life, if not one's destiny. Control requires maintaining a network of people for support in the time of need and securing sufficient private property in land such that one does not rely upon the outside for loans.[3] Loans from kin are preferable to loans from banks or loans from nonkin. The kinsperson who is in the best position to lend money and provide work for unemployed kin is the person who owns a farm.

The bottom line for practitioners of the Kentucky way is that work tasks are oriented toward meeting basic needs without overconsumption or conspicuous consumption. One afternoon in a produce stand the size of an 8 by 10 shed, people were talking about how "we don't want for anything; we live high on the hog." People are very sophisticated in knowing how to obtain "everything we need and more."

A subtle but distinct ideology of equality is part of the Kentucky way. It appears in statements such as, "We're all kin here." A highly respected judge in the region told me that "it takes awhile to become accepted here, but once you are, people take you in as family." It is not that people do not recognize differences in income, education, and skill but that these differences are not emphasized. People's resistance to specialization—the fact that they remain generalists ("a jack of all trades")—contributes to egalitarianism. On a more subtle level, the ideology of equality operates in the form of people's willingness to give freely and generously of their time and resources to help kin and neighbors on a regular basis, not just in times of crisis. University students whose families grow burley tobacco are expected to go home to help out with the harvesting and processing of tobacco regardless of how pressing their academic responsibilities might be. Needless to say, there are conflicts for many people who grow up with the Kentucky way. Work responsibilities must be compatible with and must fit in with responsibilities to family. People make constant adjustments to accommodate family needs in accordance with the basic exigencies of livelihood.

In sum, the essence of the Kentucky way is not a romantic notion; it is fundamentally practical—meticulously tailored to fit the local economy, ecology, and family structure. Preparedness is essential to the Kentucky way. It is positive and represents a great deal of foresight and planning. In order to be prepared, people marshal resources (including labor through kin networks) and knowledge to deal with a range of eventualities. In the face of plant closings, plummeting tobacco subsidies, a less and less adequate minimum wage, and the seasonal vagaries of agricultural cycles, the Kentucky way represents both continuity with past forms of rural economic organization and some creative solutions to what are becoming widespread economic conditions.

## CONCEPTUALIZING THE REGION

For purposes of analyzing the persistence of multiple livelihood strategies, I have conceptualized the region[4] in three parts, which in analytical terms can be described as follows: deep rural ("the country"), shallow rural (the area in between "the country" and "the city"), and urban ("the city"). It should be emphasized that the terms "deep rural" and "shallow rural"—even the term "urban"—are not used by the people in the region. I have devised the terms "deep rural" and "shallow rural" for purposes of understanding different kinds of livelihood patterns and opportunities for livelihood in the region, as well as variations in those patterns. Since people use different sources of livelihood in different geographical spaces, we need a way to conceptualize the space in the region. Some of the same institutions, but also some different ones, organize economic activities in the deep rural, shallow rural, and urban areas.

This analysis uses ethnographic material collected in the deep rural and the urban parts of the region to reflect upon the persistence of multiple livelihood strategies as they exist in the ethnographic present in the shallow rural. Most of the field research focused on the conglomerate of rural homesteads, factories, and marketplaces in the shallow rural. The deep rural represents the recent past of the shallow rural, that is, what life was like before industrialization. Of course, the deep rural is and has been undergoing rapid changes too, especially as farming has become mechanized and as the federal tobacco subsidies have declined in recent years.

While this book focuses on the shallow rural part of the region, the relationships between the three parts should be understood in terms of a dynamic system of multiple livelihood strategies in which people move within the region, regularly using resources in deep rural, shallow rural, and urban areas. The movements are by no means random; neither can they be understood in a single line or trajectory. People move in steps, in arcs, and in circles. They move back and forth between workplaces, they move around from one marketplace to another, and they maintain connections with their deep rural homeplaces. All, or some part, of a family network, may move from a large farm in the deep rural area to a smaller farm or homestead in the shallow rural area, but the family will spend weekends back in the deep rural area working on the family farm. The adults in the family may hold jobs in an urban area for a period of time, after which they work exclusively in the shallow rural, while they still maintain ties to the country and the city. The individual life course will have bearing on the character of the movements.[5]

Much has been written about waves of migration from the rural parts of Appalachia (Philliber and McCoy 1981; McCoy and Brown 1981; Pickard 1981), and indeed most of the people in this book are migrants. Using life histories, especially work histories, provides the key to people's spatial movements as well as their economic and social roles in family networks. Since people move often within the region, work histories provide a composite picture, indicating how individuals combine different kinds of work tasks as they proceed through the life course. Individual life histories must be understood in the context of three-generation family networks whose members are spread throughout the region. Indeed, all of the members of family networks exhibit multiple livelihood strategies that, in the best of circumstances, dovetail with the strategies of other members.

## THE SHALLOW RURAL

Why do we focus on the shallow rural area? The shallow rural is the most problematic, as well as the most interesting part of the region. It is an unstudied, unnamed, and uncategorized gray area between country and city that contains the most intricate mix of possible livelihood strategies. Both the marketplace system and the factories for temporary wage labor are located in the shallow rural; so too are small farms and rural homesteads with gardens. Significantly, no folk term exists for the shallow rural. It is not the city, but neither is it the country. The shallow rural is a predominantly rural segment located geographically between the deep rural and the urban parts of the region. People who live in the shallow rural have easy access to the resources of both the country and the city and have made the conscious choice to reside in the shallow rural rather than in the country or in the city. People who live in the shallow rural are migrants from the deep rural parts of the region. Some have chosen their places of residence because of their location directly on bus lines to their homeplace in the country. A person who speaks country English is not at all conspicuous in the shallow rural; in the city he or she may easily be labeled a hillbilly. By the same token, speakers of city English are conspicuous as outsiders in the factories and marketplaces of the shallow rural parts of the region. Urban Appalachians are migrants from either the deep rural or the shallow rural. People talk about moving to the city. Many never do; they prefer to stay in the shallow rural.

The shallow rural itself is quite diverse economically, although culturally it is relatively homogeneous, since its people identify with the country. In the shallow rural, most people still have access to plots of land sufficiently large for agrarian holdings: either small farms or subsistence/truck gardens or both. This middle ground also exhibits a complex infrastructure of highways, as well as considerable numbers of factories, shopping malls, housing developments, and mobile home parks. It is the primary location of a system of rotating periodic marketplaces and a series of factories in which temporary wage laborers are employed. The shallow rural encompasses forms of capitalist enterprise as well as forms of resistance to capitalism.

This study begins with a set of life histories of people from the community of Brandywine, the county seat of a remote rural county in the deep rural part of the region. Focus then shifts to the shallow rural, for which the most numerous as well as the most extensive series of life histories have been taken from three settings in the shallow rural: a small hamlet, a regional periodic marketing system, and a series of factories employing predominantly temporary wage labor. These settings are not in any sense equivalent; they are related because people use all three settings to generate their livelihoods. The third set of life histories are psychiatric case histories of Appalachian adolescent girls who have been hospitalized in an urban university teaching hospital. These extreme cases represent breakdowns in the multiple livelihood strategy system in ways that have serious psychiatric implications. Taken collectively, the life histories presented throughout the book illustrate changes in the complex of multiple livelihood strategies through the life course of individuals and families. Gender roles, especially the economic importance of women as their work and family activities change through the life course, receive special attention. Women figure prominently in the life histories presented throughout this book. Relationships between mothers and daughters, especially the psychological, social, and economic dimensions, have been highlighted.

One point to mention is that the division of labor by sex exhibits rather remarkable continuities from deep to shallow rural. Women and men contribute comparable, although not identical work to ensure the maintenance and reproduction of kin networks. In these life histories, multiple livelihood strategies change in content but not in form. Strategies become more problematic and difficult, but the multiplicity never disappears. Neither does the importance of the family network diminish, even though keeping the family network intact may become more and more difficult depending on the specific geographic and institutional arrangements.

There are intricate connections between the livelihood strategies in all three parts of the region. The unit of economic organization, the family network, remains stable in spite of the considerable geographic mobility of its members. The extremes of urban and rural represent not only contrasting life-styles, modes of livelihood, and forms of human interaction but ultimately the power differentials between urban centers and rural peripheries. Language differences are very poignant and quickly realized examples—country English communicates a host of stereotypes. Using it in the urban context immediately conjures up the negative image of the hillbilly and renders a person powerless (McCoy and Watkins 1981).

The people in the region refer to its deep rural parts as the country and to the urban parts as the city whether the actual city is Cincinnati, Lexington, or Columbus. Indeed, for all practical purposes, the deep rural counties constitute the remote "counties of origin" for all Appalachian migrants. Small subsistence farms predominate in the deep rural areas, although many people combine both farm and off-farm work. Some commute distances between 50 and 100 miles or more on a daily or weekly basis in order to maintain homes in the deep rural areas while working in the city. In fact, the rural and urban economies are closely related if we understand these economies in terms of the kinds of complex institutions that maintain livelihood processes.

## THE CONCEPT OF MULTIPLE LIVELIHOOD STRATEGIES

The concept of multiple livelihood strategies is itself complex. Most simply, however, multiple livelihood strategies refer to people performing many kinds of work tasks in a given day, week, season, and lifetime. The notion that a person begins a job, works for 30 years, and then retires from that job in leisure is foreign to the concept of multiple livelihood strategies. For people who practice the Kentucky way, leisure is tantamount to idleness. It is not just that people hold many jobs in the course of a lifetime, which they do; in addition to the jobs or occupations that people hold, they also perform many other work tasks for which they may or may not be paid. People are not moonlighting in the conventional meaning of the term. They could be said to have several sidelines, but often it is difficult to determine which is the main job and which is the sideline. The concept of multiple livelihood strategies is, thus, more complex than any notion of occupational pluralism (Cohen 1978:457; Löfgren 1980:211), although the idea that people work multiple jobs is certainly an important aspect of multiple livelihood strategies in Kentucky.

Most important, the concept of multiple livelihood strategies is meant to indicate that people participate in a mix of economic institutions whether they reside in the deep rural, the shallow rural, or the urban part of the region. They switch from one form of economic organization to another with great ease and for different purposes. The switching may occur in a given day, a season, a year, or in a lifetime. At different points in the life course, people work in different kinds of economies. These economies not only involve various work tasks and work schedules, ways of organizing labor, forms of equivalencies for goods and services, but they also interdigitate in complex and changing ways with one another, and they change constantly over time.

Livelihood strategies consist broadly of subsistence strategies and cash-generating strategies. In order to understand these strategies, three different kinds of economies (which are themselves complex in that they are composed of several different and interrelated principles of economic organization) can be seen, again for analytic purposes, to operate in the region: an agrarian economy; a marketplace economy, that is, a system of periodic marketplaces; and a wage labor economy that is primarily but not exclusively factory based. The agrarian and the marketplace economies each have subsistence and cash-generating sectors. People need cash to purchase items that they cannot obtain in any other way. In comparison with cash-dependent urbanites, most people operate with very little cash because they buy only what is most basic; they do not consume things for the sake of consumption. In fact, they resist conspicuous consumption.

From an analytical perspective, the concept of multiple livelihood strategies involves the life course of the individual in the context of the family network. At any given point in time, an individual may, for example, work on a farm and in a factory; he or she may also be part of a family network in which some members work exclusively in the agrarian subsistence sector and others work exclusively in the wage labor sector. Still other members of the family may "specialize" in "flea marketing," as the people put it. They generate cash as well as goods in trade. All of the members contribute something to the maintenance of the family network. Over the life course, individuals may work in all three sectors. Questions, such as "What do you do for a living?" require long and complicated answers. It does not suffice to say, "I am a ———." Pressure to assign a single occupational identity to people remains strong, however.

## THE ANTHROPOLOGICAL APPROACH

If the central questions of this book are: (1) how are multiple livelihood strategies organized; (2) how do they work; and (3) how are they both persistent and changing, then the tools of the anthropologist are ideal for dealing with these questions. The comparative, cross-cultural perspective that deals with livelihood processes, not as unique configurations but as patterns with expected variations, is a perspective that is distinctly anthropological.

Having studied rural agrarian economies from many parts of the world, anthropologists have the advantage of knowing the range of possibilities both in the composition of the livelihood strategies themselves and with reference to the variation in their organization. So much of the literature on agrarian economies assumes, however, the household to be the basic unit. Here it is not the household per se that is the unit of economic organization. Rather, the unit of economic activity is the regionally dispersed family network. The goal of economic activity is the provisioning of this unit. The economy is family oriented. Families can organize work performed by members who may live at opposite ends of the region.

The models and concepts devised here for the purpose of organizing the data have involved a constant interplay between theory and data, between concepts and the so-called facts. Indeed, what we considered to be facts changed almost as rapidly as the livelihood strategies of the people in the region. The models and concepts constitute anthropological tools for working with our data: life histories and folk concepts about family, work, and making ends meet. Concepts of kinship, residence, and household, as they have been used in the Appalachian context, are discussed in chapter 4.

To summarize thus far, this study is about work and families in an Appalachian region. It is about family networks and the ways they organize and maintain multiple work tasks—their positive as well as their negative survival strategies in the face of migration to the city, powerful urban culture, and the attraction of rural homeplace ties (Opie 1977). What happens when people succeed in making ends meet, and what happens when they do not? Understanding the struggles and the ingenious combinations of occupations and jobs pieced together seasonally and throughout the life course by families whose members may reside at opposite ends of the region is a study in management styles, coordination skills, and channels of communication. Just to scratch the surface of the Kentucky way is an enormous undertaking.

## RESEARCH PROBLEMS, QUESTIONS, AND ASSUMPTIONS

Rather than attempting to present a definitive picture of livelihood strategies, this analysis is designed to document and raise questions about options for livelihood for working-class people whose rural origins and family base are not even one generation removed.[6] It is about the viable and the not so viable alternatives for making ends meet. As such, it is designed to enable readers to reevaluate conceptions of work and family in the context of a complex and changing situation in which exist the contradictory processes of industrialization and deindustrialization, urbanization and resistance to it. How do people marshal resources, family, and neighborhood support systems in different parts of the region: farms and gardens, factories and marketplaces, communities and an urban teaching hospital's inpatient adolescent service? In the last chapter, I describe some of the possible and serious psychiatric consequences for Appalachian adolescents when these support systems break down.

That the unit of study is a rather large region has presented some special challenges as well as some special opportunities for research and analysis. The region is predominantly agrarian with small holdings. Only 2 percent of farms in the region are larger than 500 acres. There are no coal mines; nor has mining of any sort played a significant part in the regional economy. Since, even with our team of researchers, it was impossible to cover the region in any complete sense, research sites had to be selected carefully; key informants were invaluable guides for our fieldwork. It was necessary to keep very close to our research problem: that of examining the persistence of multiple livelihood strategies of people whose families move around in the midst of a rapidly changing economy. This research problem required traveling around the region and demanded the examination of the relationships between the different arenas used by people to generate their livelihoods. Thus, it was not sufficient to look only at small farms, or only at factory-based wage labor, or only at activities in the marketplaces. While it was certainly tempting to write a book about each of these, it is the relationships between these different sources of livelihood that provide the focus of this study and are critical. These relationships are brought into sharp relief by people's life histories.

The research began in a remote rural community of small-scale subsistence farmers in Brick County, Kentucky, where burley tobacco was declining as the major cash crop. There we used the records kept in the county courthouse, and in addition to our work with the people in the community, we spent time with the county agricultural extension agent. Since the family of one of the graduate students on this project had lived in Brick County for several generations, we used their connections to meet people in the area and to familiarize ourselves with patterns of livelihood in this deep rural community. Initially, we examined the impact of mechanization on the production of burley tobacco, especially the ways in which the adoption of machinery changed the contributions of women and elderly family members to tobacco production. What had traditionally (before 1950) been an egalitarian division of labor according to age and sex changed so that women and elderly people had virtually no productive role after mechanization. For decades burley tobacco had been produced using the labor of all members of the extended family without the help of machines. In the course of the research, it became clear that tobacco production was only one of many tasks necessary to maintain the household. It was also not the only source of cash.

The existence and the importance of family-oriented multiple livelihood strategies was not a recent development. For decades livelihood strategies consisted of a subsistence and a cash component in rural areas. The particular sources of cash, the size, and the labor available to work the farm and garden were variable, however. Contrary to popular belief, people in the deep rural areas in this region were never full-time farmers. Rather, people in the deep rural communities had long been used to juggling multiple tasks—on and off the farm—depending upon the season, the needs of the household, and the capabilities of individual family members as they moved through the life course. Many of the productive activities are neither wage work nor salaried work. Conventional definitions of "a job" do not adequately describe the many and varied work tasks. Odd jobs or "hacking around" occupy a great deal of people's time, especially for men. These tasks are also not recorded in labor statistics or in estimates of the gross national product (GNP). The existence of multiple livelihood strategies in the shallow rural part of the region is a form of continuity that is both a transformation and a variation upon a preexisting pattern. In the urban setting, for many families, multiple livelihood strategies are still necessary, but they become difficult, if not impossible, to maintain.

The second, and major, research site was a series of bustling marketplaces, commonly known throughout the area as flea markets. The marketplaces are located along the interstate and county highways in the area between country and city that we have called the shallow rural. I learned of these markets from people in Brick County, many of whom brought their garden crops to the market either to sell or to trade for manufactured goods, farm tools, Christmas gifts, and so forth. The markets are reminiscent of marketplaces found throughout the world—in Mexico, China, India. Their colorful arrays of fruits, vegetables, trinkets, tools, crafts, and clothing attract people from all over the region. I did not realize until the research had progressed considerably that these marketplaces are indeed quite similar to those found in the Third World. Moreover, they provide not only ready cash for the sellers but also essential items of subsistence at considerably reduced prices to people who depend upon cash for the bulk of their livelihoods. The sights and sounds of crowds of buyers, combined with the pervasive textures of smoke, fried food, bright lights, and sellers hawking their wares creates a feeling of excitement as well as a certain urgency for those trying to acquire their weekly household needs. I was warned at the outset that people would be reluctant to talk with us in the marketplaces because they did not report the money they earned to the Internal Revenue Service. Also, unregistered guns were being sold in the marketplaces. Ideas about informal economies began to form at this point, for these marketplaces were clearly outside of the mainstream capitalist economy. Yet at the same time, the activities in the marketplaces and the goods sold there are related to the capitalist economy in complicated ways.

Men in bib overalls who looked as though they came from Brick County and who, we knew, used the guns for hunting were indeed quite visible as sellers and, to some extent, as buyers. I soon learned from informants that no one was concerned about crime related to gun sales; as we shall see, all of the gun traders know one another. On weekends particularly, we also saw "city people" shopping for the latest bargains in antiques. In the beginning of the fieldwork, we were, perhaps, most self-conscious in the marketplaces. We did much observing and were careful about our questions, since every time we spoke, the fact that we were not from the country was apparent from both our verbal and our nonverbal communications. We were strangers in a world in which all of the sellers, and many of the buyers, seemed to know one another by name; many were kin.

The people who frequented the marketplaces as buyers and sellers live in the shallow rural on small farms or on homesteads with substantial gardens. Virtually everyone had at least one relative living on a farm in a deep rural area, and these relatives presently held other jobs or had been employed in a variety of endeavors at various points in their lives. Young adults worked in factories, as truck drivers, and as waitresses. They did odd jobs such as auto repair, painting, house rehabilitation, refurbishing, and construction with their siblings and cousins as well as with their fathers, grandfathers, and uncles. Most often there were several family members involved in these endeavors. We began to notice patterns of trading, exchanging, bartering, buying, and selling that had been described in many of the community studies of rural Appalachia and of the rural United States as a whole (West 1945; Stephenson 1968; Hicks 1976; Beaver 1986). I had seen some of these patterns in Brick County.[7]

Curiosity about the linkages between markets and farms was further aroused upon attending an auction next to one of the intermediate markets. Truckloads of old farm tools were being auctioned together with used toys, baskets, vases, picture frames, dishes, and so forth. Fathers and their adult sons appeared jointly as sellers at the auctions. Many of the adult men held jobs in nearby factories. The buyers attending the auction were more varied, but older men and women were commonly seen, and they appeared to know one another. It soon became possible to formulate basic questions and hypotheses about how and where people bring their goods to sell, and where the best location is for buying used goods for refurbishing and subsequent resale. The patterns of livelihood that were gradually unfolding were not simple. The timing of work and its organization—which members of families work on farms, at auctions, in markets, or in factories became critical questions. For example, how much gardening, hunting, and fishing versus how much selling in markets or work in factories will see a family through the year?

The third research site was a hamlet in the shallow rural part of the region. This gave us a residential, albeit not a community, context within which to begin to understand multiple livelihood strategies. Hamlets, small and unnamed settlements, are segments of communities. The life histories we collected in the hamlet reflect patterns of livelihood that are very similar, if not identical, to the patterns exhibited by the life histories collected in the marketplaces and the factories.

It began to be clear that what had been learned in Brick County was only the beginning of our understanding of multiple livelihood strategies. Farms, factories, and marketplaces were interrelated in this region; the task was to determine how people managed to make ends meet in a constantly changing economic environment in which factories were opening and closing and marketplaces were expanding.

Finally, the attention to urban Appalachians needs some explanation. Chapter 10, entitled "The Breakdown of Multiple Livelihood Strategies," describes two nuclear families, both of which have migrated from the deep rural parts of Kentucky and Tennessee to Cincinnati's urban Appalachian community. These families did so, however, in a manner atypical of migrants throughout the world. That is, they had migrated from a rural area to a city in which they had no kin.

The research was done in the context of an extreme situation: adolescents who had been hospitalized and placed in a urban psychiatric unit. We were interested in the cultural and economic factors, as well as in the family disruption that led to serious illness. A major clue to unraveling the psychiatric case histories came when we discovered the families' bilocal residence pattern. The nuclear families of the patients were traveling back and forth between their urban residences and their deep rural homeplaces of origin as often as 12 times per year, that is, once per month. They were trying to live in two places. The significance of the region was underscored once again. But more important, it became clear that even in the urban context where, presumably, jobs are available, multiple livelihood strategies are necessary, although they are difficult to maintain. People continue to use both the agrarian and the wage labor economies. The logistics of maintaining multiple livelihood strategies become difficult, however, especially for adult women whose extended families remain in the country.

# *Fieldwork*

*"One of these days . . . ," he was always saying. "One of these days we'll git that land back. One of these days you'll go off to school and come back and help your people."*

*Giardina (1987:18)*

Doing fieldwork in one's own backyard, so to speak, presents some special challenges—organizational, psychological, and personal—as well as some special opportunities (see Stephenson and Greer 1981). The challenges concern our proximity to the field site and the constancy of our work there. The logistical aspects of managing fieldwork proved to be relatively easy in that we did not have to travel a long distance to enter the field, experience the culture shock and the "total immersion" of a foreign culture, and then reenter our own familiar culture. At the same time, once the project was fully under way, there was a sense in which we were never absent from the field. In this respect the field was omnipresent. It was always there in some form: a phone call, a student who was going home on the weekend to harvest tobacco, or an article in a local paper that needed to be followed up. The special opportunities concern the speed with which it was possible to zero in on large bodies of data. I am still amazed at how much data we gathered and even more amazed at how much we could have gathered if we had had a larger team of fieldworkers. This gold mine of data then presented the challenge of sorting and sifting through large amounts of information.

The fieldwork in this part of Appalachia can best be described as nontraditional fieldwork for several reasons. The fieldworkers on this project operated as a team that included both undergraduate and graduate students in anthropology, as well as people from the region who often played dual roles as informants and fieldworkers. As is fitting in a complex society, we established a complex division of labor among the members of the field team. The undergraduate students focused almost exclusively on collecting data in the periodic marketplaces. They spent most of their time talking casually with people and counting types of items for sale. They also made approximations of the ages of people in each booth in order to determine the generational depth of families. The graduate students collected and organized many of the detailed life histories and helped analyze the quantitative data. Since speaking non-country English, as we came to call it, always attracted attention, the subtleties of people's reactions to us were a constant topic of conversation in our field team meetings.

The period in which the fieldwork was conducted for this project was quite extended, and to some degree it is still open-ended. It began in 1983 with the field project in the deep rural community in Brick County, and while it has ended officially, I received phone calls and letters from people in the northeastern Kentucky region during the entire time I was writing this book. Because the fieldwork was so extended, it was possible to witness firsthand changes in many aspects of the regional economy. Marketplaces grew and changed. Marketplaces, especially the small minor markets, were created, and then they disappeared. Factories closed. People took on wage labor jobs. They quit or stopped for a while and were rehired only to quit again. People were married and divorced, then remarried.

Third, the fieldwork was not conducted in a small-scale face-to-face community situation. Nor were the spatial boundaries critically important at the outset of the study. While most people confined their economic activities to the 10-county region, many did not. We became aware of the fact that there were many local, regional, and national circuits for market sellers. One circuit used by marketplace vendors encompassed Florida to the south, Michigan to the north, and Indiana to the west.

The fieldworkers moved constantly back and forth between the field and the university. Moving in and out of the field gave us a renewed sense of how different the Kentucky way really is from the culture of the city and the university. People not only spoke a different dialect of English but their expectations of one another revolved around their families and their land. They are connected to one another in ways that are unknown in most cities. People dressed differently, especially the adults and elders: bib overalls and simply cut dresses were the norm for people over the age of 45. Our comings and goings also heightened our awareness of how people were integrated into and connected to the regional and national economies and cultures. For example, teenage girls could buy clothing made by Forenza (the brand sold by the chain store,

The Limited) at a great discount when the clothes were no longer fashionable in the city. All sorts of goods could be found in the marketplaces. We saw many of the sellers in different marketplaces, and we tried to follow them around the region.

Our movements in and out of the field kept the project focused and also allowed it to shift its emphasis from time to time. Originally, I had set out to conduct a study that focused exclusively on the marketplace system. I wanted to examine its relationship to the maintenance of family farms in the area. While the marketplaces are certainly fascinating, it quickly became clear that they were tied into many other aspects of the regional economy. Certain aspects of the marketplaces had to be set aside. In sum, the movements between the field and the university also obviated a feeling of total immersion and isolation in the field that has for so long been one of the hallmarks of anthropological field research. There were substantial benefits to be had from this kind of fieldwork, however. Interaction with colleagues, anthropologists, sociologists, and psychiatrists was of great benefit. Students could also join the project at various points in time.

## FIELDWORK IN THE MARKETPLACES

Because the marketplace sites are open, public places, they were always accessible. These marketplaces, known to the people as flea markets, are a system of markets that are hierarchically organized in terms of size and volume of business. We could go to the markets whenever they were in operation. The accessibility of the marketplaces proved to be tricky, however, for it did not necessarily mean that information was easy to gather, or that it was easy to locate people week after week. Markets seem, at first, to be constantly changing groups of people; yet once the schedule of the marketplace system became apparent, certain vendors could be followed systematically.

Talking to the vendors revealed that people sold goods in many markets in the region. Following the vendors presented some real logistical problems, however. How, given our limited number of fieldworkers, could we cover so much territory? Since the marketplaces were spread over a north-south trajectory of over 120 miles, we were forced to make some difficult choices, many at the last minute. Once an understanding of the schedules of individuals became easier, we could plan our movements.

Initially, the fieldworkers entered the marketplaces as buyers, a role that was comfortable for beginning student ethnographers. The arrangement was also convenient because produce could be obtained very cheaply and was easy to buy, since its quality could be quickly judged.

The produce vendors were among the most aggressive of the sellers. They would literally follow a person down the aisles. Since everyone in the marketplace is so busy, people are easy to observe without having the fieldworker feel too conspicuous. Interactions with people are short, however, and often several visits were necessary in the same day if one really wanted to talk to a particular vendor. From the outset the field-workers controlled many elements of the fieldwork situation. On any given market day, vendors are stationary. Fieldworkers had time to plan their movements within a marketplace. For example, one day we might choose to focus on the vendors of used items alone; another day we might concentrate on the vendors of new items. We might spend the entire day talking to and observing one of these vendors. Other days we covered more ground and observed patterns of selling and buying such as the relative proportions of new and used goods. Usually we did both, and this was one of the advantages of working in a team or in pairs. Often, however, vendors did not have time to talk.

Vendors we came to know in the marketplaces became key informants whom we visited outside. I remember a visit to Amy and Mike (see chap. 8), who are market vendors as well as tenant farmers. As soon as we arrived, they went inside to change their clothes. They offered us food and ice tea, and then we sat under a tree in their front yard for several hours. While we were there, their landlord, Mr. Wainright, came by to talk to Mike about his work on the farm. The landlord was openly critical of the quality of Mike's work. When the landlord left, we talked about Amy and Mike's relationship to Mr. Wainright. We asked about him because he made us feel extremely uncomfortable. The landlord had seemed to want to talk to us as though Mike and Amy were not there, even though Mike identified us as "his friends."

The pace of our conversation was leisurely, however. Mike talked about his stint in the military and how he went to the city to get completely drunk the night before he left for Vietnam. Children and family occupied most of the conversation. One of the fieldworkers talked to Amy about Mike's infidelity and the fact that he is a brash fellow who wants to get rich quick, while the other fieldworker chatted with Mike about horse breeding. After our talk they took us on a tour of their farm. We saw their house, garden, and livestock. We never felt rushed or that we were occupying too much of their time. We did, however, feel an obligation to reciprocate their hospitality and generosity—that we should contribute something to their livelihood. Before leaving their place, we bought five dozen eggs from them.

Many aspects of the marketplaces could be observed in silence. These observations provided extremely important data—data every bit as valuable as that gathered from interviews. We learned a great deal simply by watching, listening, and counting. Among the things we counted were the numbers of cars and the numbers of license plates by county that were found in the parking lots of factories and markets. We also counted the numbers of booths and kinds of goods—new and old—at each market each week. We constantly checked what people told us against what we observed. The sheer number and variety of economic activities was often astounding and a bit overwhelming at times.

Indicators of the pervasiveness of the Kentucky way were observable in almost every booth. In one sense people were selling the country by marketing what people take to be symbols of wholesomeness, cleanliness, and simplicity. Traditional wash basins were for sale, as were quilts. While some of these had been manufactured as pseudoantiques, there were also many actual antiques, most of modest value. For example, depression glass and small pieces of wooden furniture such as chairs and tables were common. Wooden bins marked with the word "taters" conjured up images of Grandma peeling potatoes. One vendor told me, "There is a lot of country stuff here."

The marketplaces themselves are completely unspecialized. Many booths have a plethora of things, both old and new. A newcomer to the marketplace would have a difficult time seeing everything in one booth, much less the range of goods available in the entire marketplace. To an outsider the variety, the noise, and the seemingly chaotic movements of people in the marketplaces can prove bewildering, but the sellers themselves always seem to be calm. Grandmothers sit on rocking chairs against the far walls of the booths eating stewed tomatoes and beans from Tupperware containers. Only the children buy hot dogs and french fries from the concession stands. Marketplaces are bustling places, but they are not frantic; people are busy, but they do not rush. Constant work is carried out, and idleness is rare. People bring their handiwork. Women prepare pieces for quilting; they knit and work with embroidery. Men fix tools, small appliances, and machinery; they bring woodcarvings. People do not look at their watches constantly. They do not measure the length of their conversations.

Political messages could be seen in the marketplaces, if one knew where to look. Confederate flags associate people with the Old South. Honesty prevails. People trust one another, and the same sense of neighborliness described by many in rural communities operates in the marketplaces. People help one another by watching each other's booths. Stealing is not a problem. Sellers are all extremely generous in helping customers. Two teenage boys patiently taught my (then) five- and six-year-old sons to set their new $3 digital watches. There is an atmosphere of friendliness that communicates more than "we want to sell you something." Commercialism, while certainly present, is underplayed. At the same time, my questions pertaining to the source of the watches fell on deaf ears.

Trust is communicated by indicating one's willingness to talk and spend time. Only then does one become part of the information system. There is also an air of reserve—of people checking one another out. Therefore, politeness is extremely important; people go out of their way to use perfect manners. You also must indicate, somehow, that you identify with at least some of the same things, with some part of the Kentucky way.

Most conversations deal with families and land. Where a person lives, that their goal is either to secure land for themselves or to find a way to hold on to family land—these are prime topics. For example, one woman told us about how her dad bought land for her. Houses, repairing homes, adding on to existing structures, children, and grandchildren— all of these topics indicate that a person identifies with the importance of home and family. One woman described in great detail the illnesses of her daughter-in-law. At first we dismissed the details as irrelevant to the study of livelihood. Then we realized how the idiom of the family worked. The more details one provides, the more one exhibits caring for a family member—thus caring about family in general. People begin by asking, "Who are your people?" This provides the entrée for them to talk about "my people." The folk term for kin network is "my people." The word "people," of course, is plural, but ambiguous because the exact number is open. "My people" can contrast with "my family," which has a discrete folk meaning in this context and refers to a person's nuclear family. The confusing point is that people use the term "family" in several ways. It can mean nuclear family, but more often the term "family" is used more broadly to mean kin network. It will become clear that when I use the term "family," I am using it in the broader sense to mean kin network.

It is through talk about "my people" that people talk about themselves. In other words, the kin network is the idiom that people use to talk about themselves in a culture in which talking about one's self directly is "bragging." When people talk about "my people," they are communicating their priorities, especially that they have a set of people upon whom they can rely. Often people will tell a stranger about a member of their family. But what they are actually communicating is the importance of the family and thus their country identity, the importance of the Kentucky way in all of its ramifications. Therefore, talking about "my people" is a way of presenting and representing oneself as part of a larger entity. It communicates a kind of anti-individualism by immediately contextualizing the individual in a larger grouping, in this case, a kin network. It indicates that the person, in fact, has a network.

Situating oneself inside a network indicates that one has access to labor resources and probably to land as well. When people meet, there is an immediate sorting out of who is related to whom. In the marketplaces people constantly are waving hello to one another and calling one another by name. There is an air of familiarity. A person wins prestige by revealing his or her kin network, for the network is his or her resource base. People talk negatively about people without kin. People who are alone are objects of pity.

Gender was an important factor in fieldwork. Women will talk more easily to other women. Men speak to other men. In order for men to talk to women fieldworkers, either another man must be present or the man's wife must be present. These experiences gave us our initial clues to how sex roles operated in the culture. It is extremely important to know whether or not people are married. Adult women and men are supposed to be married. Once married, people are expected to have children. People do not ask about plans for children because being infertile is also "a pity." Children are still important as labor, as insurance, and as more family. The frying pan is a symbol of the division of labor between the sexes; it is also joked about as a weapon—a woman's weapon.

There were instances where the discussion of finances, a male domain, became tense. Asking a working-class man questions about an area that is perceived to be personal would, in many instances, cause tension and even conflict. I remember being driven around the countryside one day by Wendell and Charlotte, for whom the drive constituted a good excuse for an outing. The couple occupied the front seats of the car; I sat in the back seat with one of the student fieldworkers. We had just finished lunch ("dinner" in folk terms) at a charming old restaurant in the deep rural part of the region, where the old soda fountain and the original cash register were still in place. The menu reflected the best of authentic country cooking, and the beverages came in old glasses with Coca Cola written on them in script. Wendell took great pride in showing us the countryside, almost as though all of it belonged to him.

I knew that Wendell had been working odd jobs with his brother for some time. I also knew that he had had a series of temporary wage labor jobs. I was not quite sure what kinds of odd jobs he had been involved in, and since he seemed rather relaxed, yet in full control of the situation—quite literally "in the driver's seat"—I took the opportunity to ask him some rather pointed questions. He and his brother had been renovating houses. Some of the work had been obtained through a contracting company. He had also told me that he had done some other jobs "on my own," and I was extremely curious to know about the work in detail. He appeared to regard the work with a certain casualness—even flippancy—which aroused my interest all the more. On the one hand, he seemed proud of his control of his working life and of his partnership working with his brother; on the other hand, he seemed to want to convey the impression that he did not regard the work with any degree of seriousness. When I asked about how long the renovations would take, and whether the work was difficult, he told me "not very long; it's easy work." Yet, at least at this particular time, it occupied the better parts of his days. I could not help but think that he was purposely downplaying the work because he was not declaring the income for tax purposes, or he felt that from my point of view it was not a "real job." Because he seemed ambivalent toward me and my questions, I decided to pursue the issues a bit further. He had mentioned a job refinishing floors for a woman in the next town, a job he had obtained through his uncle. "How much can you make on that floor?" I asked him directly, to which he responded, "It's none of your business." I could see and feel his wife cringe. From that moment on, my interactions with Wendell were stylized, even ritualized. He not only resisted my questions but all that I represented to him—the urban life.

Since the majority of the fieldworkers for this study were women, there is a gender bias. We definitely had easier access to the female domains of culture. For example, we know more about mother-daughter relationships than we do about fathers and sons. We could talk to women about their relationships with their mothers, but in most instances, we could only observe father-son relationships. In fact, a friend of a young woman, whose case history is presented in chapter 9, wrote to me specifically to tell me that Winnie, who is about to remarry, is looking frazzled. She has been busier than usual because her mother broke her leg, and Winnie took over "Mom's role." Winnie's youngest brother remarked to her one day that he had not realized how much work his mother had to do each day and how much he missed her "working" around the house. As for Winnie's mother, who had never been sick before, "bein' laid up" just about drove her crazy. Winnie said that "not working gave Mom a lot of tension." As soon as Winnie's mother could stand, she was back in the kitchen cooking supper. She was also back buying things in the Redside marketplace, one of the largest in the system.

The marketplaces are, in many respects, an ideal arena for observing relations between the generations. It is not uncommon to see all three generations of the family in a booth (see Appendix). Adults spend time with children, and children have important functions in the marketplaces. They help customers, and they watch over the merchandise of other booths as well as their own. They talk to their grandparents. They run errands. In the marketplaces children find themselves in the midst of an adult world; they are expected to work along with everyone else because special concessions are not made for children. The generational division of labor in the marketplaces is reminiscent of that found on the self-sufficient family farms in this area.

Factories presented a very different fieldwork situation; it was impossible to gain access to the factories themselves. Because industrial espionage is a significant issue in the area, all workers, including temporary wage laborers, were required to sign statements promising not to talk to anyone outside of the plant about their activities at work. The guarding of "trade secrets" and the fear that the competition would steal important information were the reasons stated by the companies for these required statements. We learned about the factory work primarily through key informants; since we were not at all interested in the technical aspects of the work, we did not present conflicts for the workers. Actually, people wanted very much to talk to us about the Kentucky way, especially about how they decided to take one job or to leave another. Again, in this context as well, people expressed their feelings about the importance of kinspeople. Even though the work was short-lived, workers, particularly women, clearly established some very strong ties with one another in the temporary workplaces. One woman, Lydia, described finding a co-worker crying in the women's washroom during a break. The woman was crying because she had just been notified that her job would terminate at the end of the week. "She has no family left in the country," Lydia explained. "All of her people have gone to the city, and they have no garden."

## FIELDWORK ON AN INPATIENT ADOLESCENT PSYCHIATRIC UNIT

Being the anthropologist on an adolescent, inpatient psychiatric unit, a locked ward requiring one to use a key to enter as well as to exit, proved to be a moving, as well as an enlightening, experience.

The nurses, especially the "primaries" (often a licensed practical nurse), were our main data gatherers, since they spent the greatest amount of time interacting with the patients. Their sensitivities, their powers of observation, and their abilities to articulate the patients' problems produced literally mounds of data. Their level of intimate knowledge was impressive.

The adolescent unit itself functioned on a team model of treatment. Members of the treatment team included the attending psychiatrist (who acted as the head of the team), psychiatric residents, psychiatric nurses (RNs) and social workers, secondary-school teachers, art therapists, and medical students. Their approach is multidisciplinary. As the anthropologist on the unit, I attended treatment team meetings, during which the patient's progress, medications, length of stay in the hospital, and whether or not to send the patient to a treatment home for adolescents were all discussed. The adolescent unit clearly had a culture of its own, with its own rules. Again, it was tempting to take detailed ethnographic field notes on the unit itself. The research problem, however, was to try to understand the relationships between Appalachian culture, family structure, and livelihood strategies in the development of psychiatric disorders among adolescents.

The nurses, and other members of the treatment team, were wonderful informants. They expressed great interest in Appalachian culture; many of them had worked with Appalachian patients at the hospital or in nearby clinics for several years. Together with the attending psychiatrist on the unit, I worked closely with the nurses who had been involved with giving treatment to the two young Appalachian girls whose case histories are presented in chapter 10. The choice of two female patients for inclusion in this book is in keeping with our discussions of mother-daughter relationships. The mothers of the patients played key roles in both the illnesses of their daughters and in the treatment of the illnesses. The particular social and economic circumstances in which the mothers found themselves upon moving to the city also contributed to the progress of illness. Of particular note is that both mothers moved to urban areas where they were without kin. All of "their people," were left behind in "the country," that is, in the deep rural parts of Tennessee and West Virginia. These areas are not, strictly speaking, part of the region under study, but they are similar enough to the deep rural counties in the region. The one exception is that the West Virginia deep rural community is in a coal-mining area.

As it happened, one of the nurses who worked on the adolescent unit came from an Appalachian background. She demonstrated a very special sensitivity to the importance of the extended family in general, and of grandparents in particular, in supporting the livelihood strategies and the psychological well-being of rural migrants. It was she who was able to question one of the patients in such a way that the young girl "opened up." That a nurse of Appalachian origin was able to achieve such a breakthrough raises some important issues for training health care practitioners and anthropologists. How could we use her folk knowledge about the importance of the family networks, for example, to train the residents and child psychiatry fellows? What were the similarities and differences between Appalachian patients and other patients from lower socioeconomic backgrounds? What are the racial, ethnic, and class components of psychiatric treatment? As one of the residents put it, "How do you know culture when you see it on the unit?" (This question has haunted me ever since I heard it.) What are the key elements of the Kentucky way that are most useful in clinical settings? Is it possible for health care practitioners to learn enough about "peasant wisdom" so that they can acquire the same, or at least similar, sensitivities to those that come so naturally to the Appalachian nurse?

*The flat landscape of northeastern Kentucky*

*Rolling hills*

*A typical tobacco barn*

*Livestock in the deep rural*

*A footbridge*

*Tobacco drying*

*A subsistence garden*

*A church in the shallow rural*

*A subsistence garden*

*A yard sale*

FOUR

# Historical and Anthropological Overview

Many scholars have noted the failure of their peers to treat Appalachian people tolerantly or evenhandedly (Keefe 1988; Bryant 1979, 1981, 1983). The negative stereotypes have been applied to migrants and nonmigrants alike (Weller 1965; Ball 1968; Caudill 1962, 1971, 1976; Toynbee 1947; McCoy and Watkins 1981). Appalachian people have been victims of the same kind of labeling and stereotyping that has been experienced by other minority groups. Some of the labels may sound more "down home." But other labels, such as "barbarians," "yesterday's people," and "hillbillys," are more blatant pejoratives. Still other pejorative treatments are more subtle, but in the long run, more damaging to the image of Appalachian people and to the ways in which they are treated by health professionals, educators, policymakers, and other "helping" professionals. The work of child psychiatrist David Looff, whose book *Appalachia's Children* (1971) still stands as a classic in American psychiatry, is an example. His failure to understand the nature of kinship ties in rural cultures (blaming "overly close families" for school phobias and other disorders) has been transmitted to several generations of mental health professionals. The power of the concept of the culture of poverty is still with us, despite the numerous critiques of that concept almost two decades ago (Leacock 1970; Stack 1974).

Scholars are just beginning to address heterogeneity within the Appalachian culture area. While there is no question that Appalachian people have experienced political, economic, and cultural domination, the assumption has been that their response has necessarily been negative (Gaventa 1980; Whisnant 1980, 1983; Lewis 1978; Walls 1978).

I want to examine some of the ways in which analysts of the Appalachian region have dealt with the problem of the livelihood of kin and to provide a brief historical overview of the region.

By reviewing concepts of kinship, family, and household, clear pan-

Appalachian patterns in the organization of livelihood by kin throughout the region can be made visible. At the same time, transformations of and deviations from those patterns are occurring through the maintenance of the Kentucky way, for it involves continuities as well as transformations and reinterpretations of kin and community in relationship to livelihood. Probably the most remarkable aspect of the Kentucky way is that it operates, for the people in this study, outside of traditional community contexts. The Kentucky way involves an expansion of the range of kinship ties and an expansion of the tasks of kin network members. It also involves an expanded sense of what is local (local refers to a region, not a community or even a county), while enabling people to maintain a strong sense of locality. Locality has clear referents to deep and shallow rural counties and their relationships. What is local does not include the city. I want to clarify that I am using the terms "family" and "familial" to refer to an extended network of people who are related by blood or marriage, that is, consanguines and affines. Family refers then to kin and to kinship relations in a bilateral sense. I use the terms "family network" and "kin network" interchangeably to emphasize the point that the terms "family" and "kin," as I use them here, do not necessarily imply coresidence. It will become clear that people mobilize ties to family members in the region as a form of outreach to people with diverse skills, knowledge, experiences, and resources. One part of the family network quite literally "holds on to the land" (Hall and Stack 1982), while others engage in a diverse set of livelihood strategies yet always maintain the option of coming back to the land, either temporarily or permanently. The most important point to realize is that the goal of economic activity is to sustain the family network (Bott 1957).

The portion of the Appalachian region under study here has certain distinctive features as well as definite shared characteristics with other areas of Appalachia.

## KINSHIP IN APPALACHIAN COMMUNITY CONTEXTS

Kinship has always figured prominently in Appalachian studies. The strength of family ties and the importance of the land, both for material and psychological security, have been discussed by many scholars. Since most studies of Appalachian culture have been community based, kinship has been analyzed in community contexts. Beginning in the early 1940s, James Brown (1952) studied family groups in a southeastern Kentucky farming community. He found the family groups, which consisted of several households, to be community-based groups descended from an original settler. The family groups engaged in numerous cooperative activities that included reciprocal cooperative labor for farming and household tasks, housebuilding, trading and lending of tools, and so forth. Meals were shared; life crises were given social and psychological support through visiting; and help with child care was provided. Following Brown's studies, Marion Pearsall conducted a community study in eastern Tennessee (1959), where she found similar patterns of family groups with a community basis. Later studies by John Stephenson (1968), George Hicks (1976), and Carlene Bryant (1979, 1981, 1983) observed family groups in community contexts.

Family, land, and community have become something of a holy trinity in Appalachian studies. Patricia Beaver writes of the breadth of kinship and of the interconnectedness of kinship and local identity:

*Kinship and family in the rural mountain community are a highly valued and central part of life. Yet kinship is more than biological or genealogical connectedness, it is a cultural idea through which relationships are expressed and from which community homogeneity is derived. Kin ties connect community residents into a system that gives personal identity through the expression of common roots, common ancestry, shared experience, and shared values; kinship also provides an idiom for people's behavior toward one another and is one of several bases for the actual formation of groups.*

*(Beaver 1986 : 56–57)*

Historically, too, family, land, and community have been closely associated. Land has both economic and psychological significance and provides security in both domains. In this context familism is not isolating or insulating, it is part and parcel of a rural way of life. Ronald Eller writes:

*Land held a special meaning that combined the diverse concepts of utility and stewardship. While land was something to be used and developed to meet one's needs, it was also the foundation of daily existence giving form to personal identity, material culture, and economic life. As such, it defined the "place" in which one found security and self-worth. Family, on the other hand, as the central organizing unit of social life, brought substance and order to that sense of place. Strong family ties influenced almost every aspect of the social system, from the primary emphasis upon informal personal relationships to the pervasive egalitarian spirit of local affairs. Familism, rather than the accumulation of material wealth, was the predominant cultural value in the region, and it sustained a lifestyle that was simple, methodical, and tranquil.*

*(Eller 1982 : 38)*

As a cultural idea, kinship can be played out or expressed in many ways, including the organization of economic activities and economic relationships in nonresidential contexts. As Alan Batteau (1982b: 447) has noted, however, most of the traditional studies consider the importance of kinship in the life of individuals or families, but not in the structure of larger political units. Also, he points out that we have little information on the larger context of these communities, and thus we do not know whether the kinship systems reported by these ethnographers are "isolated happenstances" or whether they are typical of the region.

Batteau's own study, in an impoverished area of the Cumberland Mountains, also focused on aggregates or clusters of kinspeople descended from a common ancestor and living on or near the original homeplace. He calls these aggregates of kin "sets," and he reports that when asked what a set was, people say: "A man raises his family, and his children raise up their families right around him, and *their* children also raise up their families there. That would be a set" (Batteau 1982b: 448). He also notes instances, however, in which the households of three siblings (sisters) were several kilometers apart. Yet since the households were on an all-weather graded road, people could drive from one household to the other in five minutes. In the more remote areas, however, clusters of siblings and their parents often resided together in the same hamlet. The intensity of interaction was considerable. Batteau quotes one old man from such a residentially based kin group: "Me and my daughters and the old woman, we kind of live through and through one another; what one's got, the other's got." He reports that these families planted a garden together, and midday meals were taken in the most convenient household. Although financial resources were not pooled, the households were closely linked by financial assistance, loaning of tools and appliances, and outings to stores taken together.

In a summary statement, Batteau says that the set should not be considered as a concrete, bounded group, but rather as "a core resource for network formation" (1982b: 451). He minimizes the economic importance of sets by saying that people can "claim kin" by belonging to the same set. That is, they can "invoke obligations of kinship, including sociability, political support, and minor economic assistance" (1982b: 451). For Batteau, the establishment of residence at or near the original homeplace is the key relationship that defines the set; residential patterns perpetuate sets. He says, "The set is a conceptual map orienting action, rather than a consistently valid description of behavior. Based on kinship, locality, and reputation, it provides an orientation for certain key relationships among the mountain people" (1982b: 451). He concludes by saying that the set is "a predominantly rural phenomenon: in areas where land is bought and sold commercially, one does not find sets" (Batteau 1982b:451). Here our data show a somewhat different pattern. Family networks remain intact as cooperating economic units, despite an increasingly commercialized environment. As we shall see in chapter 6, which focuses on a hamlet in the shallow rural, residence patterns are found that are similar, but not identical, to those described by Batteau. With one exception, segments of extended family networks live in the hamlet. Other segments live in different hamlets, or in the deep rural areas. In an extreme case, the entire family network resides in a single hamlet in the shallow rural. Our case histories of market vendors corroborate the dispersed residence pattern for extended family networks that are units of economic organization. In other words, what Batteau calls "sets" exist in the shallow rural, but not as residential units.

## HOUSEHOLDS AND APPALACHIAN COMMUNITY STUDIES

Households are, and have always been, basic units of the economy. In Appalachia they are also basic economic units. Maintaining the household, feeding its members, and caring for its dependents are probably cultural universals, at least in state-level societies. Households are also visible, physically bounded units that are relatively easy (once one gains entry) to observe, to count (census data are based on households), and to measure in relationship to one another. Recently there has been a resurgence of interest in the household as a unit of study and analysis among many scholars (Elder 1981; Laslett 1972; Hammel 1972; Maclachlan 1987; Netting, Wilk, and Arnould 1984). In Appalachian studies, households have also figured importantly. It is essential to understand exactly how households have been used in the Appalachian literature in order to understand the potentials as well as the limitations of the household as the unit of economic analysis. This is especially important, since family networks often involve several households that are dispersed throughout the region and whose relationships with one another are the key factors in maintaining the Kentucky way. Batteau has contrasted the domain of householding with the domain of kinship in Appalachia. For him, households are bounded units containing nuclear families: "A nuclear family occupies the house, and it is thought improper for more than one family to live under one roof. The household is very tightly bounded: Strangers, including fieldworkers, have to be very careful about how they approach the house. . . . The house is the normal place for eating meals, and very rarely will unrelated families sit down together at the same table to eat" (1982a:33).

The typical residence pattern as described by Batteau is for parents to live in one house and for the houses of their married children to cluster around the main house. For Batteau, the domain of householding is "a set of relationships based on coresidence, commensality, and fixity of place. Its emphasis is on independence, sharing within an independent unit; yet the continued dependence within a family, carrying through even to the establishment of new domestic units, is also clear" (1982a: 33).

Batteau proceeds to contrast the domain of householding with the much broader domain of kinship: "We can see how this domain of householding contrasts with the domain of 'pure' kinship. 'Pure' kinship emphasizes solidarity between all persons related by blood and marriage and a certain identification with them; householding emphasizes independence. The conjunction of the two is the structure of the hamlet, in which the children's homes may be as little as ten yards away from the parents' yet still be structurally separate" (1982a: 34). The pattern of physically separated households interlinked by ties of dependency upon kin is a common pattern throughout Appalachia. We know also, however, that even as residential units, there is considerable variability in household composition and size, especially with the seasonal migration of adult males and with temporary additions of kin (Hicks 1976: 36).

All of this research points to the limitations of the household as the unit for analyzing livelihood. In many economies, households would tell us a great deal. In this eastern Kentucky region, however, households tell only part of the story when it comes to understanding complex patterns of livelihood, partly because household composition is so fluid. Mothers and daughters move easily between households: mothers perform services for daughters, and daughters reciprocate in kind. Married children and their spouses share meals regularly with their parents, even though their households may be as far apart as five to 10 miles. In short, the relationships between nonresidential households are critical; these are cooperative relationships between households—interhousehold cooperation outside of community contexts. As we shall see, cooperative relationships are played out in the marketplaces; it is common to see representatives of three generations in market booths at the same time. The members of these families do not reside in the same household, nor do they reside in the same community. In all likelihood their residences are spread within the shallow rural; in many cases some members of the families live in the deep rural. If we do what Netting and his colleagues (1984) suggest and examine what households do, we find that they are dispersed throughout the region as parts of family networks; that they play a part in a rather complex division of labor for the group; that division of labor changes as the group goes through its developmental cycle (Goody 1958, 1972, 1976). In northeastern Kentucky, households are units of economic cooperation, but they are not the only units, or even the most important units (Arcury 1984).

The critical question is, How can we use the descriptions and analyses of family-organized economic activities to understand patterns of livelihood among kin, that is, making ends meet, the Kentucky way? The intellectual context within which one understands the operations of familial economies is critical for our analysis. Analysts Billings, Blee, and Swanson (1986) have argued that what older, more traditional writers Pearsall (1959), Stephenson (1968), and, to some extent, Brown (1952) "saw as *antiquated* behavior were traces of a social logic and a set of values distinct from those of more advanced capitalist societies but nonetheless shaped by economic rationality" (Billings, Blee, and Swanson 1986:156). Their argument, one that is certainly applicable to the northeastern Kentucky region, is predicated upon an enlarged contemporary vocabulary that talks about relations of power—resistance and accommodation, class formation and class antagonism. Their notion of rationality is based upon a broader idea of the logic of economic systems than that restricted to a Weberian calculus of quantifiable gains. They elaborate, "The mountain people's indifference to the rituals and desires of an industrial society was consistent with their life of self-sufficient production and local networks for consumption. The muted hierarchies of worth and achievement were reflective of a social stratification system still shaped as much by mutual exchange as by competitive gain" (Billings, Blee, and Swanson 1986:156).

Presenting a somewhat different, but no less complex, view of mountain economies is a recent discussion by Jeff Titon, who says, "Although they kept to their household economies, the mountain farmers' mindset was by no means anti-commercial. They were acquisitive and held commercial values and expressed them; but their orientation was largely non-capitalist. They understood trade, and they knew commercialism through their dealings with the marketplace (read market system)" (1988:131). While the argument is still based on the household as the unit of economic analysis, it is important because it takes into account the relationships among rural agrarian economies, commercialism, and capitalism. It does not assume that commercial elements automatically indicate a capitalist system.

The continuities between family-organized economies in the mountains and those in the deep and shallow rural parts of Appalachia are quite striking. The dynamics and intricacies of these family-organized economies are just beginning to be explored, however. These are not traditional, primitive, kin-based economies; they operate in a commercial, capitalistic world. Nor are they capitalist enterprises. Given the juxtaposition between commercial economies and noncapitalist production systems, familial economies present considerable challenges for analysis. In contrast to the coal-mining areas, where people may become dependent upon cash and perpetually indebted to company stores, people in the deep and shallow rural parts of this region of northeastern Kentucky may never become cash dependent. This is true of many people who maintain ties to land and family. More important perhaps, people who entered the wage labor market took care to maintain their local agrarian knowledge.

## A WORKING DEFINITION OF THE FAMILY

In 1974 Carol Stack published *All Our Kin*, a study of kinship and exchange networks in a black ghetto community outside Chicago. She was among the first anthropologists to write about the family outside of household contexts. In that book she set forth a working definition of the family that I have always found useful for its cross-cultural applicability. I present below a modification of that definition for purposes of understanding family networks as organizers of complex livelihood processes outside of both household and community contexts.

The cross-cultural definition of the family as I have modified it from Stack's work is as follows: The family is an organized, durable network of bilateral kin who may or may not reside in a given locale or household. These people see it as their responsibility to provide for the needs of family members, especially dependents (both children and seniors), to assure their well-being. The advantage of this definition is that it does not make any assumptions about residence patterns. Most important, it allows for the family network's flexibility, its change in size, function, and location. Family networks are, in northeastern Kentucky, durable and flexible. Depending upon the needs (especially the labor needs) and the resources of individuals or groups within the network, the number of people involved "as family" will vary. In general terms, in agrarian subsistence economies, the family is more likely to be found in one locale, so that there is a high correlation between family and community. This gives a residential base to the network. Where the family farm is the unit of production and consumption, as was the case in the deep rural parts of our region up until about 1950, all three generations resided in a common settlement and sometimes, but rarely, in the same household. There was, and still is, complementarity and mutual dependence between the generations. Elderly people perform important management, production, and food-processing tasks. Older women supervise food processing for both storage (canning) and consumption (cooking). Depending upon their age and sex, children also play vital roles in subsistence economies. They run errands, help with the harvest, take care of younger children, gather berries and firewood, and so forth.

What emerges in our region is a complex, familial economy composed of networks of kin. The kin network organizes labor and allocates resources, but now in a nonresidential context. People coordinate their economic activities by performing such services for one another as cooking, shopping, and doing laundry. They also care for the old and sick.

The relationships between household units and the property of kin is complicated. Once they are married, young adults live in their own households, whether these units are houses in the same community as the parent, or whether the units are mobile homes or apartments somewhere in the region. People have access to the services and many of the goods of others in their kin network. People may use fruits and vegetables, for example, from gardens on their parents' land. They also have access to washing machines, stoves and cooking equipment, and to stored foods.

The economic ties between kin in this region are not sporadic or idiosyncratic; they are regular and patterned. They are not just a matter of remittances or of seasonal movements back and forth from agrarian to industrial sectors. Rather, there is both long- and short-term contact between kin who work in different economic sectors—regular and sustained contact among kin for economic purposes: production, distribution, and consumption.

The following example of a segment of a family network in the shallow rural part of the region illustrates the ways in which the nonresidential family network organizes and coordinates economic activities in the agrarian, the marketplace, and the wage labor economies. I have chosen this family for several reasons. First, they are typical of numerous regional families in that their family network encompasses many people and extends throughout the 10-county region. Multiple livelihood strategies are well illustrated by this family, since its members participate, or have participated, in all three economic sectors: agrarian, marketplace, and wage labor.

## COORDINATING MULTIPLE LIVELIHOOD STRATEGIES

Harry and Ilene Smith (both in their sixties), along with their daughter, Sue, and son-in-law, Nathan, are planning their economic activities for a fall weekend. Harry and Ilene live in one household in a shallow rural hamlet; Sue and Nathan live with their two children, a four-year-old son and a six-year-old daughter, in another household in a mobile home park six miles from Sue's parents. The following activities need to be coordinated. Harry has two house-painting jobs to finish before the weather turns cold; he also has several indoor house-renovating jobs. He and Ilene are regular vendors in the periodic marketplace system, and they are eager to sell off the goods they have accumulated over the summer by attending garage sales and auctions. The best day to sell at the Redside Market, a major marketplace in the system, is Saturday or Sunday. Ilene is also very concerned about "putting up" her beans and cucumbers for the winter; if she does not process them in time, both beans and cucumbers will grow too large and tough to be eaten. Ilene's sister is ill, and Ilene must take some cooked food to her sometime during the weekend. Sue and Nathan also work as temporary wage laborers in a nearby factory: they work six days each week on varying shifts and sometimes work double shifts.

Ilene and Harry decide to sell at the Redside Market on Saturday, the busiest day. They take their grandchildren with them. Sue and Nathan will harvest the beans and cucumbers and prepare food to take to Ilene's sister after work on Saturday. On Sunday they will all go to Sue's aunt's farm in the country for their Sunday dinner.

We can see from this case the ways in which people select and coordinate elements from the agrarian, marketplace, and wage labor sectors. They do so by using the schedules of the members of the family network to the best advantage. There is time flexibility in the agrarian (subsistence gardening) sector that is not possible in the wage labor sector. The marketplace sector is flexible with regard to child care, although the schedule is not. Therefore, Sue and Nathan may exchange child care for their labor in the garden during hours when they are not involved in wage labor. The different workplaces present different kinds of opportunities as well as different kinds of constraints for members of the family network. Combining the different workplace activities gives people control over scheduling and also allows them time to care for family members. At a later date, Sue's aunt will provide Sue and Nathan with farm produce.

The northeastern region of Kentucky, Ohio, and Indiana must be understood in the context of the Appalachian area as a whole. At the same time, the region's distinctive features must be recognized: there are no discernible mountains; there has never been coal mining; and people own land. Despite the emphasis upon coal mining that has appeared in the media, Appalachia has always been predominantly agricultural. Small-scale farming has remained the primary economic activity with low levels of technology and little mechanization on any scale. Some have argued that historically Appalachia has also been agricultural in spirit. "Such industry as existed tended to be periodic, seasonal, or occasional, to be highly decentralized, to be dependent upon low capital investments except for raw materials (as land for timbering, mining, and, of course, agriculture), and to require occupational skills which were essentially continuous with those already possessed by an agricultural population" (Shapiro 1978:162). That the region under study is not a coal-mining area, but rather an area of small subsistence farms adjacent to coal-mining areas, renders its features and its history much more similar to areas of North Carolina (Beaver 1986) than to many other areas of Appalachia, including West Virginia, Tennessee, and other parts of Kentucky.

Before the early 1970s, when small industry began to move into the region, it was an area of small subsistence-oriented family farms with burley tobacco as the major cash crop (Van Willigen 1989; Axton 1975). Growing burley tobacco is extremely labor intensive and requires substantial numbers of people to participate in virtually all of its many stages of production. Beaver notes that burley tobacco production is particularly suited to "the fluctuating mountain economy" and to part-time farming, but it is a crop that requires relatively small amounts of land and limited equipment (Beaver 1986:34). Burley tobacco production operates in this region of northeastern Kentucky in a manner similar to that which Beaver describes for North Carolina. Tobacco chores can fit in with other kinds of off-farm work. Tobacco is an important supplementary source of income for many rural families (1986:34).

The 10-county region of northeastern Kentucky is difficult to characterize in simple terms. It is still dominantly rural and agrarian, with an economy historically based on small family holdings. This ties it to an overall Appalachian pattern. Pockets of industry can be found in the northern shallow rural part of the region. Yet visually the area appears to be much like other parts of the rural United States; it is not dramatic in any way. The landscape is relatively flat with gently rolling hills. The shallow rural has its share of superhighways and fast food restaurants, whereas the deep rural does not. Tobacco warehouses, now flea markets, are very visible. Many people talk about the marketplaces as though they were still the old warehouses. In the shallow rural, traffic can clog the superhighways for considerable distances when shifts change at factories. There are a few relatively affluent suburban bedroom communities in the shallow rural.

The deep rural can best be described as a bucolic setting. It has a different, Old World feeling—almost as though it is part of the European countryside. The towns are village-like. Everyone knows everyone else by name and by family. Old buildings that date back to the turn of the century and before are still common. Some households have only recently acquired electricity and indoor plumbing. In spring, yard sales in front of houses on country roads often exhibit goods belonging to several families. Roadside stands contain local produce—corn, tomatoes, squash in the summer and apples and pumpkins in the fall. During the fall, golden tobacco leaves hang in barns. Small farms with barns can be found on winding roads, where people wave to those passing by. People are calm and friendly. On the smallest roads, vehicles must pull off and stop to allow a car or truck coming from the opposite direction to pass. Signs announce the names of towns, cities, and hamlets, although one should not take the word "city" too literally. Church steeples dot the landscape throughout the region, particularly in the deep rural. Some hamlets have as many as three churches, but every hamlet has at least one. Hamlets vary in size, containing as few as two or as many as a dozen houses. Hamlets can be found in both the deep and the shallow rural.

A county seat is recognizable by its rather imposing, generally brick or stone, county courthouse, surrounded by a post office, some shops, perhaps a restaurant or two, and a general store. Feed stores and signs that advertise farm insurance and farm equipment provide a distinctly rural flavor to the entire region. Although the educational system is consolidated into county-run schools, one can still see one-room schoolhouses standing in the deep rural areas. Population figures reflect lower population densities in deep versus shallow rural areas, as well as lower per capita incomes. Table 1 shows the range of population size for deep and shallow rural counties in the region. Table 2 shows per capita income in the region by county.

## ECOLOGY

The 10-county region that is the focus of this book lies in the northeastern part of Kentucky. The area is characterized by gently rolling hills; the elevation does not exceed 1,000 feet above sea level. The region is dominated by the Ohio River on its northern border, with several tributaries and a great number of small creeks. Forested areas are primarily deciduous secondary growth.

The climate in the region is temperate. Temperature extremes range from an average summer high of 97.3° F to a winter low of −1.38° F. The mean annual temperature is in the middle 50° F. Precipitation is relatively constant throughout the year, with monthly averages ranging from 2.95 inches to 4.64 inches of rain. Average annual precipitation is about 46 inches. The growing season, or number of days between each frost, is relatively long at an average figure of 183 days.

Brick County, a typical deep rural county, had a total population of approximately 7,500 in 1985. Its county seat had 700 people, down from 800 in 1952. The total population in the county in 1952 was 8,468. Organized in 1796, the county was named for a pioneer who visited the

**TABLE 1**
**Population of 10-County Region**

| Deep Rural Counties | 1985 | 1984 | 1980 |
|---|---|---|---|
| Randolph | 2,200 | 2,300 | 2,270 |
| Stone | 17,200 | 17,300 | 17,760 |
| Wool | 10,900 | 10,800 | 10,989 |
| Brick | 7,500 | 7,500 | 7,738 |
| Knight | 4,900 | 4,900 | 4,482 |
| Granite | 14,000 | 14,000 | 13,308 |
| Ford | 15,800 | 15,600 | 15,166 |

| Shallow Rural Counties | 1985 | 1984 | 1980 |
|---|---|---|---|
| Daniel | 51,400 | 50,200 | 45,842 |
| Canter | 80,900 | 81,500 | 83,317 |
| Kerry | 137,200 | 136,700 | 137,058 |

territory in 1773. The county is situated in the tier of counties located along the Ohio River in the east-central part of the state. The river provides the northern border with many small creeks that traverse the county. The land surface ranges from rolling to hilly; mineral resources consist of limestone, used for construction purposes, and residual clay, used for brick manufacturing. The elevation of the county ranges from 480 to 925 feet. Soil is fertile in this county. Even steep hillsides can be planted in corn, tobacco, and alfalfa. Bottomland is, of course, the most fertile. In this county the chief cash income is from burley tobacco, but dairying, beef cattle, sheep, and poultry also generate cash. Enough hay is grown to satisfy local needs.

Ninety-six percent of the 131,840 acres (206 square miles) of land in this county is farmland. In 1950 the population density was 41.1 people per square mile. In 1940 there were 1,370 farms averaging 91.8 acres; in 1945 there were 1,480 farms averaging 83.3 acres; and the 1950 census lists 1,364 farms averaging 92.8 acres. The 1945 figures show a larger number of farms with fewer acres. This difference can be attributed to a change in the definition of "farm" from one census period to another. Many small tracts were classified as farms in 1945 but were no longer classified as such in 1950. Usually, any tract under three acres is not reported as a farm unless the agricultural product value is more than $250. This dollar value brought in many tracts under three acres in 1945, but these were not included in 1950. In 1950 there were approximately 225 farm wage laborers in the county, and 500 unpaid farm family workers. By 1978 there were 803 farms.

According to the 1950 census, in 1949 approximately 11 percent of the farms produced less than $600 total value of product; 8 percent, less than $1,000; 29 percent, less than $1,500; 52 percent, less than $2,500; and 74 percent, less than $4,000. Of the total product, anywhere from 20 percent on some of the larger farms to almost 100 percent on some of the small farms was consumed on the farm by farm family members. Income must maintain and improve the farm, pay taxes and insurance, buy farm supplies and equipment, and provide a living for the farm family. Wages in 1951 ranged from $3 to $20 per day. Generally, wages were paid at $.50 to $1.00 per hour.

The following statement about industry and economic development was written by farm service people associated with the Kentucky Chamber of Commerce in a 1952 report on a deep rural county:

**TABLE 2**
**Per Capita Income in the 10-County Region**

|  | 1983 | 1979 | % Decrease |
|---|---|---|---|
| Randolph | $5,548 | $4,392 | 26 |
| Stone* |  |  |  |
| Wool | 6,593 | 5,152 | 28 |
| Brick | 6,948 | 5,014 | 39 |
| Knight | 7,091 | 5,531 | 27 |
| Granite | 7,166 | 5,648 | 27 |
| Ford | 7,107 | 5,369 | 32 |
| Daniel | 9,079 | 7,200 | 26 |
| Canter | 8,443 | 6,564 | 28.6 |
| Kerry | 8,891 | 6,867 | 29 |

*Figures not available.

*Opinion is much divided on industry. Some believe industry would make labor harder to get. Others think it might be good for the county. Many think it is needed. The feeling generally is not too enthusiastic. Some think it would be all right if it would employ people only when they are not needed on the farm. Some believe there should be industry so that poor and rough land would not have to be farmed. Industries most favored were a fertilizer plant, a plant to process farm wastes, clothing manufacturers and textile plants, sheet metal plant, cannery, or other industry employing women. Some think that industry would be good for one of the larger towns, but would not be good for the rest of the county.*

*Many of the ideas advanced above indicate good thinking on the part of some of your people. Generally speaking the interviews indicate a lack of solidarity and desire for community cooperation among the people and the absence of a unified approach to general economic development.*

In comparison to coal-mining areas, the region in which we conducted research has been exploited on a relatively low scale by outsiders. In fact, the distinction between insiders and outsiders is difficult to draw in the area because most people in the region view themselves as migrants of one sort or another. Outsiders can also be kept out of kin networks and hamlets in ways that they cannot and have not been kept out of mountain communities.

In the nineteenth century, the cities along the river in the shallow rural areas provided homes to German immigrants who worked and established small factories and businesses. At the turn of the century, a steel mill, several breweries, a locomotive plant, and a foundry were among the industries located there. In 1921 a strike in one of the steel plants, a major employer of river city residents, caused the composition of the shallow rural's population to change. The owner of the plant brought in people from the mountains to work in the plant. Many of the mountain people were of English, Scottish, and Irish origins, and their descendants are the people who live by the Kentucky way.[1] Some linguistic carryovers in the form of common expressions that derive from Gaelic are, for example, that people talk about "belonging to the country." Gaelic-speaking Scots use the same expression: "I belong to [the town of] Lewis" (Kerry Skiffington, personal communication). The German Roman Catholic population gradually shifted to a Protestant Fundamentalist population. In the late 1980s, the same steel plant employs between 800 and 1,200 workers. People have understood for decades the fluctuations in the plant's need for labor. They realize that layoffs are a possibility, and they plan accordingly. They know and have known that work in steel mills will not provide a secure livelihood.

# NONCAPITALIST ECONOMIC PATTERNS IN THE REGION

In general, the region as a whole follows a pattern of small holdings, many of which historically have operated outside of the market (system) economy. Between 1800 and 1900, two basic noncapitalistic economic patterns[2] emerged in the Appalachian region (Precourt 1983:90). They are, in Walter Precourt's terms, family-based subsistence farming and independent commodity production. These patterns should be understood as models, that is, idealizations of what actually exists, and variations of these patterns still exist.

## Family-Based Subsistence Farming

The first pattern can be understood as family-based subsistence farming. In 1880 Appalachia contained a greater concentration of noncommercial family farms than any other area in the nation (Precourt 1983:91). Following Eller (1982), Precourt uses the term "family enterprise" to describe the all-encompassing nature of family-dominated economic activities. The whole purpose of the enterprise, however, is not profit but meeting the needs of the family. When goods were purchased or sold by these enterprises, the aim was still to maintain the family. While the following description refers to farms in the mountains, it can readily be adapted to the northeastern Kentucky region. It is in effect a description of agrarian units in the deep and shallow rural parts of the region prior to 1950: "Each mountain homestead functions as a nearly self-contained economic unit, depending upon the land and the energy of a single family to provide food, clothing, shelter, and the other necessities of life. . . . the family not only functioned as a self-contained economic unit, but it dominated the economic system itself. The mountain farm was a family enterprise, the family being the proprietor, the laborer, and manager; the satisfaction of the needs of the family was the sole objective of running the farm" (Eller 1979:92).

An example of a subsistence economy is that described by James West for Plainville. People spend no money for much of their subsistence: virtually everyone raises large gardens and keeps livestock. The majority of farmers raise most of what they eat, and some raise virtually everything except staples such as flour, sugar, and coffee (1945:40–41). Precourt points out that some trading and bartering was done, but these activities were not interrelated with other aspects of the economy and were not based on a commercial market system of supply and demand (1983:91). These themes are repeated throughout the Appalachian literature, albeit with many variations.

## Independent Commodity Production

Precourt's second economic pattern is independent commodity production (after Banks 1980). The main feature of this pattern, which also should be understood as a model with many variations, is that the producers, in this case families, control the means of production. Families carry out the distribution of goods without an intervening labor market and, in some cases, without a monetary system. Production and consumption are localized (Precourt 1983:91). Banks characterizes independent commodity production in eastern Kentucky during the late 1800s: "Regular household needs, from clothing and food to soap, lamp oil, spirits, sorghum, hand tools, and stoneware, were satisfied through a local trading network based upon the exchange of products from household manufacture, limited farming, and artisanship. The producers and consumers in this setting were virtually one and the same people (1980:189).

West's discussion of trading in Plainville illustrates some of the key aspects of independent commodity production—aspects that are played out in our region of northeastern Kentucky. Trading is an important form of barter through which people exchange goods (livestock, staples, etc.) and services (labor) outside the regular commercial (market) economy. In addition, it is a way of demonstrating skill in bartering, since the object of the trading is to outwit one's trading partner. West describes a long and complicated ritual of trading in which men engage in "lengthy verbal sparring and bantering; disparagement of the partner's goods, and 'brags' regarding one's own goods; numerous offers, refusals, and counteroffers; and (often) recountings of 'famous' local trades. A man is admired for trading victories, and even for deception of his trading partner, if he has only concealed or evaded reference to flaws in articles offered. Deception must follow rigid rules. To lie directly is to 'cheat'" (1945:20–21). As we shall see, the kind of finesse described here is common in trading relationships in eastern Kentucky, whether these are based in local communities or in marketplaces.

The family dominates the economic system for working-class Kentuckians. Now, however, the family-based economies described in this book operate in terms of a highly complex set of relationships to the capitalist market system. Economic activities may operate outside the market system, in opposition to it, and in cooperation with it. The complex familial economy has adapted to capitalism, and in many respects people have used elements of the market system to their best advantage.

To summarize, we can see that capitalistic enterprises certainly existed in the more urbanized parts of the Appalachian region. Although these enterprises provided jobs—and thus cash—for people, as well as outlets for certain mountain products (galax sold as greenery for flower arrangements, ginseng sold to merchants who, in turn, sold it to Chinese in New York who used it for medicinal purposes), for the most part the region consisted of family-dominated agrarian holdings. These holdings are very different from farms, as we ordinarily think of them in the Midwest. This difference was illustrated by a 1945 study by Frank Alexander and Robert Galloway, who contrasted the rural economies of "a typical county in the Northwestern Wheat-fallow sub-region of the Wheat Belt with one in the Southern Appalachian Mountain sub-region." Farming in the wheat-growing county, based on large capital investments in mechanized farming, is a large-scale operation with the average gross income in 1945 being $33,000 from wheat alone. By contrast, farming in the Appalachian county is small-scale and subsistence oriented. "A typical farmer in this county plants about half of his cropland to corn which is the basis for food for his stock and his family. . . . purchases are confined to necessities—principally clothes and a few staple foods that they cannot produce on their farm" (Alexander and Galloway 1947:396; Precourt 1983:92).

In the Appalachian literature, unfortunately, family-based economic enterprises have come to be associated with poverty. What is perhaps most unique about our analysis is that "the image of poverty," as Precourt puts it, is not at all prominent in this northeastern Kentucky region. People have continued the same pattern of family-dominated economic enterprises; they are not poor by any means, even though their per capita income figures are low.

If we look at official per capita income figures alone, we can see that people would need to have other sources of income as well as goods and services, to survive. In the deep rural counties, the average per capita income is between $4,000 and $5,000 per year. In the shallow rural, it is between $7,000 and $10,000 (U.S. Census 1983). Clearly, people have diversified into several different economic sectors. The activities in these sectors are not always measured in the per capita figures, however. The family organizes the diverse work tasks in intricate patterns, and their economic activities can be understood as both combinations and variations on the two patterns of family-based subsistence farming and independent commodity production.

In northeastern Kentucky, continuities with this past system of family-based subsistence farming and independent commodity production are abundant. Vendors in marketplaces deal in petty commodities of many sorts. Some of these commodities are home produced; others are old things, bartered things, even things gleaned from the environment and transformed by adding labor. Members of three-generation extended families are involved in the sale of commodities in combination with agrarian subsistence efforts. Members of extended family networks contribute to one another's material needs in myriad ways outside of community contexts. The intricacy of this system of family-based, multiple livelihood strategies will be revealed in the following chapters.

# FIVE

# Deep Rural Economy: Multiple Livelihood Strategies in "The Country"

*Across the hollow that divided our place from Grandpa's I could see his house and the two barns white in the sun. . . . Grandpa's farm had belonged to our people ever since there had been a farm in that place, or people to own a farm. Grandpa's father had left it to Grandpa and his other sons and daughters. But Grandpa had borrowed money and bought their shares. He had to have it whole hog or none, root hog or die, or he wouldn't have it at all. Uncle Burley said that was the reason Daddy had bought our farm instead of staying on Grandpa's. They were the sort of men who couldn't get along owning the same place.*

*Our farm was the old Ellis place. Daddy had bought it before brother and I were born, and we still owed money on it; but Daddy said it wouldn't be long before we'd have it all paid. If he lived we'd own every inch of it, and he said he planned to live. He said that when we finally did get the farm paid for we could tell everybody to go to hell. That was what he lived for, to own his farm without having to say please or thank you to a living soul.*

*Berry (1960:7–8)*

This chapter focuses on multiple livelihood strategies in a representative town from one county in the deep rural segment of the region. People refer to this part of the region as "the country." The term "deep rural" refers to a model with geographical, ecological, and cultural designations. The model is designed to indicate a part of the region that is most distant from the city and most plentiful in natural resources. People perceive living in the deep rural as the most ideal environment for practicing the Kentucky way because, from a cultural and psychological perspective, the deep rural part of the region is "home" to many people who reside in the shallow rural and the urban parts of the region.

There is, thus, both a fluid and a temporary quality to residence outside of the country (deep rural).

The deep rural parts of the region are the locations of family land, and land is at the base of the solidity that people find there. The deep rural sector of the region is one of small subsistence farms with substantial kitchen gardens. Burley tobacco is the major cash crop, but as indicated in the last chapter, all cash cropping in the region is done on an extremely small scale in comparison to most farming in the Midwest. The pattern of multiple livelihood strategies, that is, multiple sources of subsistence as well as multiple sources of cash, is the distinctive feature of the deep rural system of livelihood. We see variations upon this pattern in the shallow rural part of the region.

The settlement pattern in the deep rural is the traditional one: homesteads develop out of extended family life course patterns. As children marry, ideally they establish households on the family land. This is true, of course, if they do not migrate out of the deep rural. A household rarely contains two generations of adults (Foster 1988 : 55; Beaver 1986 : 99).

People own family land in the manner of a landowning peasantry. Land is property, and landownership confers independence as well as a sense of place. As Stephen Foster writes, "Land is also regarded as property, which persons as owners control. Possession of land assures self possession: the landowner is his or her own person, has secured a definite identity, is 'beholden to no one,' has acquired a measure of autonomy and independence" (1988 : 169). Alan Batteau makes a similar point, although in folk terms: ". . . owning a home is preferable to being 'just a renter,' for the homeowner and landowner is therefore independent; as one fellow put it to me, 'He has land that he can be independent on'" (1982a : 33). Landownership also confers control over resources, especially the labor of children. All children inherit land on an equal basis; it is not uncommon, however, for a brother or sister to sell his or her parcel of land to a sibling in order to move out of the deep rural. The deep rural community described in this chapter is much like many of the classic Appalachian communities described in the mountain areas where coal mining was absent. For example, James Brown's Beech Creek community in southeastern Kentucky is a case in point. Small, family-run subsistence farms that operate relatively self-sufficiently, with the large majority of agricultural products consumed by the producers, is the dominant pattern. As in Beech Creek, tobacco was until recently the main source of cash (Schwarzweller, Brown, and Mangalam 1971; see also Pearsall 1959; Stephenson 1968; Bryant 1981).

Life histories from the town of Brandywine, a pseudonym for the county seat of Brick County, show the features of multiple livelihood strategies, especially the importance of kin networks. The multiple livelihood strategies described for northeastern Kentucky are not idiosyncratic, unique, or deviant but rather are quite typical of Appalachian rural areas and of other areas in the rural United States and in Europe as well. Conrad Arensberg's study, *The Irish Countryman,* is particularly appropriate for comparison, given the Anglo/Irish/Scottish origins of people in Appalachia.

I want to emphasize the variety and complexity of highly localized rural economies and the links between these local economies and the regional and national economic systems (Batteau 1983). These economies were never as isolated as the stereotypes would have us believe. The intricacy and resiliency of these small-scale economies have not been fully documented in the United States. The following passage, written about another Appalachian region in which coal mining was absent, is probably the best introduction to the town of Brandywine. I quote this passage not for comparative purposes but because it captures in a succinct fashion the basic features of deep rural subsistence economies in the United States. For Appalachia, it is particularly important in light of the great emphasis that has been placed upon coal-mining regions to the exclusion of other areas. "As in many parts of the Appalachian region, especially those in which coal mining was absent, subsistence farming was the major mode of obtaining a livelihood since at least the 1930's and in our region well up into the 1960's. Even today it is not uncommon to find elderly couples who subsist primarily by planting kitchen gardens, keeping a few livestock and hunting and gathering squirrels, rabbits, nuts, berries, etc." (Montell 1986:6).

Small holdings predominate in Brick County. In 1920 the county had a total of 1,812 farms averaging 200 acres in size. Larger farms, of 500 acres or more, constituted only 5 percent of the total number of farms. This trend persists throughout the county. In 1978 there were 803 farms in the county. The average size of farms equaled 141 acres. At this time less than 2 percent of the farms consisted of 500 acres or more. The pattern in this county is fewer farms with a continued emphasis on small landholdings.

The town of Brandywine itself is typical of many rural county seats, although it is smaller than most in the region and its buildings are less imposing. The population of the town itself is 800, including eight hamlets (settlements). A small library occupies the town square along with a dry goods store, a saloon, a post office, and a fast food shop. The most imposing building of all, the county courthouse, sits in the center of the town square. This large structure symbolizes the power of the national legal system, the bureaucratic red tape, the representatives of the nation-state. Among these representatives is the agricultural extension agent, a university-trained, kindly man whose office is in an upstairs corner of the county courthouse.

Face-to-face interaction between people in the town is constant. Elderly people are "looked in on" by neighbors and kin; people are never socially isolated even if their homes are a fair distance from the nearest neighbor. Most important, people live by combining different kinds of livelihood strategies: subsistence farming and cash cropping or subsistence farming and truck gardening. Even the smallest of the small homesteads operates by using family labor in a variety of tasks that change seasonally and throughout the life course.

## SELF-SUFFICIENCY IN A DEEP RURAL ECONOMY: RUTH AND BOB

Ruth and Bob, a childless elderly couple who have been living on their land for over 50 years, exemplify the system of multiple livelihood strategies on a small and somewhat extreme scale. Because they are quite elderly (both in their eighties) and because their lives have not changed appreciably over the last 30 or 40 years, their life-style provides a glimpse of past deep rural adaptations as well as a traditional contemporary case.

Ruth and Bob live in a very small house on the outskirts of town. A stream separates their house from the road in such a way that their house can be reached only by a rickety, well-worn wooden footbridge. Their nearest neighbors, who live about a mile down the road, look in on them every few days. Adjacent to the house is a small garden and a pumpkin patch from which Ruth and Bob feed their single milk cow. Their well-trained collie guards the cow and the garden areas.

At night their house is lit by a kerosene lantern, and their stove is fueled by wood. Ruth is known throughout the county for the cakes that she brings regularly to church functions and community gatherings. She makes them from scratch using her own butter and eggs. Ruth is also the only driver of their car. They use the car sparingly, primarily to go to church, to the store to purchase staples, and for their annual visit to the physician. For the most part, with the exception of their few store-bought staples, Ruth and Bob produce what they need to live. They sell some corn and pumpkins to generate small amounts of cash as well. At one time they also worked a small tobacco plot, but they have given this up in recent years.

## THE AGRICULTURAL EXTENSION AGENT

The county agricultural extension agent is a man who speaks slowly and deliberately, as though weighing each separate word before he answers the questions of city folk. He is deeply concerned about the economic conditions in this rural area, especially now that changes in the tobacco subsidy program have rendered tobacco difficult to manage as a cash crop. He talks about possibilities for developing the bell pepper as a cash crop and about cooperative farming arrangements both for purposes of producing and distributing crops. He talks speculatively, although briefly, about craft production and fish farming. He is pessimistic, however, since the larger individual families have always fended for themselves in "the country." Also, taking crops to market from this relatively remote area is a significant problem. Roads are bad, especially in winter. He told us that for people to give up a method of livelihood such as tobacco growing is "like pullin' eye teeth." There is strong pride in the work of the generations. Tending the soil and attachment to the land is deeply entrenched. In this light the agricultural extension agent indicated his optimism. These farmers had lived through difficult times before, rather successfully; they could do it again. What he did not say, but he did imply, was that this method of livelihood was a complicated one, involving many people and many carefully timed and orchestrated tasks. Giving up this multiple livelihood strategy would mean giving up a complex and highly organized social as well as economic existence that would jeopardize the entire rural social structure.

## BURLEY TOBACCO

Burley tobacco involves both men and women working at all stages of production. Before mechanization, tobacco beds were worked by hand. A tobacco seedbed is usually nine feet wide by at least 100 feet long. The beds are worked by hand with rakes, hand sowed, and then covered with canvas. Each plant is pulled separately and bundled to be reset in a larger field. Before transplanters and tractors, tobacco was set by hand. Weeding is another laborious task performed by men and women alike. When tobacco is topped (the seed bloom broken off, a procedure that causes the plant to grow bigger leaves), it grows off-shoots of small, gummy leaves at the junction of each regular leaf where it joins the stalk. These "suckers" are not good for sale. They do not cure well, and they get in the way of removing the good leaves. Up until 20 years ago, when chemical sprays were developed, tobacco was suckered (i.e., the suckers are removed) by hand. This work was done in the heat of August. Each sucker had to be removed one at a time. In many cases there was a sucker for every leaf. Cutting the tobacco is another laborious task. Stalks were cut one at a time and speared on a tobacco stick. "Housing" the tobacco, or moving it from the field to the barn and then hanging it in tiers requires at least two people in the field to load wagons and three in the barn. The tobacco must be hung carefully on rails with just the right spacing for air curing. After the tobacco is cured for several weeks, it is then piled together to help retain the moisture that prevents the leaves from crumbling. Then the leaves are stripped from the stalk, one leaf at a time. The tobacco must also be sorted by grade. After the crop is stripped, graded, and pressed into bales, it goes to market in the tobacco warehouse (Carraco 1987).[1]

## LIFE HISTORIES IN THE DEEP RURAL

*When my parents left for Florida, Stephen and I moved into their old farmhouse, to take care of it for them. I love its stateliness, the way it rises up from the fields like a patch of mutant jimsonweeds. I'm fond of the old white wood siding, the sagging outbuildings. But the house will be sold this winter, after the corn is picked, and by then I will have to go to Louisville. I promised my parents I would handle the household auction because I knew my mother could not bear to be involved. She told me many times about a widow who had sold off all her belongings and afterward stayed alone in the empty house until she had to be dragged away. Within a year, she died of cancer. Mother said to me, "Heartbreak brings on cancer." She went away to Florida, leaving everything the way it was, as though she had only gone shopping. . . . we are in the canning kitchen, an airy back porch which I use for the cats. It has a sink where I wash their bowls and cabinets where I keep their food. The canning kitchen was my mother's pride. There, she processed her green beans twenty minutes in a pressure canner, and her tomato juice fifteen minutes in a water bath. Now my mother lives in a mobile home. In her letters she tells me all the prices of the food she buys.*

*Mason (1982: 122–123)*

The following life histories illustrate how people organize their multiple livelihood strategies throughout the life course and in the context of extended family kin groups. The histories are taken from people who have lived in Brick County for most, if not all, of their lives. They emphasize the economic links between kin, including reciprocal cooperative labor arrangements and the economic components of intergenerational ties. The ways in which kin groups combine labor for subsistence production with wage labor, and the ways the relative proportions of different kinds of labor change over time, are particularly evident in the two cases.

## Hattie Kimball

Hattie Kimball was born in 1926. She was 58 years old at the time of our fieldwork. Brick County has been home to Hattie for her entire life. She grew up there on a 120-acre tobacco farm. She lived and worked on the farm with her parents and two older brothers until she was in her early twenties. Throughout her childhood and early adulthood, men and women shared farm work according to season and age.

Hattie's maternal grandparents' farm was adjacent to her parents' farm. Reciprocal work arrangements as well as general reciprocity prevailed. Tasks shared ranged from the harvesting of crops to household maintenance and child care. They also shared leisure time. After church the extended family would gather at the grandparents' house for elaborate home-cooked meals, music, and frolic. Sunday dinner provided a break in the week and a respite from the arduous farm labor.

While in her early twenties, Hattie married a county resident who owned an inherited family business, a garage. Her marriage removed Hattie from the family farm, but not from her familial obligations. Since she was not actively engaged in the activities of the garage, Hattie worked for her relatives (aunts, uncles, and cousins). Her parents and grandparents had died, and their family farms had been sold. She felt particularly strong obligations during the harvest of burley tobacco and the postharvest season. At no time did she hire herself out as a hand. She offered her labor to her relatives with the expectation that they would reciprocate by helping her with her household maintenance, child care, errand running, and food processing and storage (canning in particular). Although Hattie has maintained her own household (which includes a substantial garden) since her early adulthood, the economic and psychosocial support offered to and by her relatives is essential. Reciprocity forms the basis for the organization of the extended family. People are expected to help one another and to provide for one another as needed. When she needed additional cash, Hattie sold some of her garden products: fresh vegetables in the summer and jams, jellies, pickles, and other "put up" products in winter.

Hattie Kimball gave birth to three children, two girls and one boy. Of her three children, the two daughters are engaged in the production of burley tobacco. The eldest daughter has a B.A. degree from a state college and taught school for approximately six years in the county school system. After these six years, however, she decided to stop teaching and

to farm her mother-in-law's farm. The former teacher was quoted as saying: "Farming is more relaxing than teaching school; it gives you more
freedom." The younger daughter farms her father-in-law's farm with her
husband. Both daughters also work off the farm by maintaining some
form of seasonal work in adjacent counties. Much of this was related to
tobacco.

Hattie's daughters' experiences in the farming of burley tobacco are
very different from her own as a girl growing up in the 1930s. Her
daughters' farm labor is a seasonal endeavor that provides supplementary wages for their household. A similar situation exists for Hattie's
son. He works in the family garage under his father's supervision for a
weekly wage. The son's dependence on the father for his wages is very
different from that shared by Hattie's older brothers who worked on
their family farm. Hattie's brothers were not dependent on wage labor
for livelihood. They could work off the farm when they chose to do so.
Hattie's son still has access to garden products, however, by virtue of his
residence in the deep rural part of the region. He does not, however,
claim any knowledge of farming.

Today Hattie is an extremely energetic woman. She maintains active
involvement in community affairs: the church (including Sunday School
teaching) and meeting her reciprocal labor obligations, and she still en-
gages in much subsistence production centered around her garden.

The freedom about which Hattie's daughter speaks is rooted in the
family-based multiple livelihood system. By maintaining access to her
in-laws' farm, she maintains not only access to reserve cash but to food
produced in gardens as well. The timing of her work, while complex and
often delicate, is still more flexible and certainly more varied than her
work as a teacher. While the requirements of tobacco production demand that appropriate and laborious productive processes such as stripping the tobacco leaves be performed within a relatively short period of
time, the decision of both daughters to remain in the deep rural area
permits them long periods of leisure if they wish. Their residence in the
deep rural also keeps them in close touch with their substantial network of kin, including Hattie.

### Beatrice Flannery

Beatrice Flannery was born in 1906 and has been a county resident all of
her life. Beatrice grew up on a 100-acre farm with her parents and three
younger siblings, two sisters and one brother. Recalling her early years
on the farmstead, Beatrice said, "Then mostly everybody had large families. You raised all you ate—like five hogs would be butchered in fall to
tide you over 'til spring. Buying knickknacks [snacks] was out. Times
was hard; we didn't have a lot of conveniences, but we were a lot happier

than today. For entertainment, we might have gone to the neighbors and popped popcorn in a wire basket over the fire, made candy, or sat around the hearth and cracked hickory nuts. Times was hard, but they was good times."

Beatrice and her entire family worked in the fields hoeing tobacco, tending the vegetables, and minding stock from sunup to sundown. Caring for the family farm was a full-time job, and Beatrice talked about how it was a real struggle for her family to pay for their farm. Both men and women participated in most farm tasks, depending upon season and upon who was available. Beatrice did point out, however, that the men's work ended at the back porch. Housework was women's work. "You'd be so tired when you came in from them fields, but you had to fix supper. Lots of time our supper was just a gallon of pole beans and some corn pone [cornbread]."

In addition to preparing the family's meals, the women of the household mended, washed, and ironed clothes. The tasks were physically laborious as well as time-consuming. Clothes were washed on a washboard, sometimes in the nearest creek if a permanent water source was not near the house. The garments were hung outside on a clothesline to dry. The women later pressed the clothes with an iron (made from actual cast iron) heated on a wood stove. They also manufactured and used their own homemade starch (flour and water). Throughout the interview Beatrice repeated, "We wouldn't have made it through all of that hard work without the Good Lord."

When she was 21, Beatrice married a county resident who was a tenant farmer. They had five children: four daughters and one son. Parents and children worked side by side in the fields. They sold tobacco and garden produce and saved as much as they could toward the purchase of their own farm. In 1948 a tornado struck the county, and Beatrice's husband and only son were killed. Beatrice could not maintain the family's status as tenant farmers, keep up with the household, and raise four daughters. She and her daughters moved in with her youngest sister, and Beatrice took a job in the high school cafeteria for a salary of $15 per week. Each week Beatrice contributed a portion of her wages to her sister's household. In addition, Beatrice helped her sister on her farm and helped in the household whenever she could, especially during periods of intensive food processing in the late summer and fall when food had to be put up for the winter. Beatrice's work in the cafeteria was grueling: 800 schoolchildren had to be fed on a daily basis. The manual labor involved was endless: peeling potatoes, hand-pressing hamburger patties, grating cabbage for coleslaw. Beatrice stated that the cafeteria work was a lot harder than the farm work in the tobacco fields.

Beatrice's daughters each developed very different lives as adults. The eldest daughter became a secretary and moved to Chicago. The second-born child went to nursing school and moved to St. Louis. Beatrice's third daughter loves tobacco farming. She maintains her residence in the county, where she works as a seasonal laborer. She lives in her own home on a plot of land large enough for a substantial garden. The garden is not an insignificant source of livelihood, as she never has to buy a vegetable. She even sells some of the vegetables during the summer at a roadside stand near her house. One farmer said that she was the best tobacco hand he had ever hired. The youngest daughter also lives in the county. She went to the state university, received her M.A. degree, and is now a teacher in the local school system. While the youngest daughter attended the university, Beatrice provided her with cash, amounting to about one-quarter of her paycheck per week; out of her $33 per week salary from the cafeteria, she gave her daughter $8.

Beatrice retired from the cafeteria in 1971, when she was 65. She now lives alone in the county, under the watchful eyes of her two daughters who are also county residents.

We can see from the life histories of Hattie and Beatrice that their patterns of livelihood and the patterns of their extended families are quite similar. Both Beatrice and Hattie have multiple sources of subsistence, as well as multiple sources of cash to purchase staples. Subsistence sources include their own gardens as well as the gardens and livestock of their extended families. Cash sources include the earnings from the sale of cash crops, from garden produce, and from wage labor.

Both Hattie and Beatrice lived and worked as children and young adults on similar kinds of farms, similar in size and organization. They were expected to share in both the farm and the household work as soon as they were six or seven. They would help mind their younger siblings, run errands, and help with household chores. Both were reared in extended family, farm households, and as young women, they were expected to perform both farm and household tasks. Beyond the farmstead, their education and socialization consisted of attending school in a one-room schoolhouse and in attending Fundamentalist churches situated in or near their hamlets of origin. In adulthood Beatrice and Hattie continued working hard on the farm and in the household. Had Beatrice's husband and son survived, the two life histories might appear to be almost identical, at least as far as livelihood strategies are concerned.

The patterns of multiple livelihood strategies for Hattie's and Beatrice's extended families are not at all uncommon for deep rural areas in Appalachia. The ways in which kin relations structure and organize rural economies, the complex economic links between kin, especially the economic components of intergenerational ties, are common throughout Appalachia and indeed typify rural economies all over the world. The various combinations of agricultural labor (both for subsistence and for cash purposes) and wage labor (seasonal labor on the farms of others as well as labor off the farm and outside the agrarian context) are also common. Exchanges of goods and services between kin and between neighbors are part and parcel of social and economic life in deep rural economies.

There are certain features of rural economy and society that are implicit in the case materials and that need to be underscored by additional comparative data. This is necessary in order to understand exactly how patterns of multiple livelihood strategies work in deep rural areas and how these patterns can be continued and maintained, albeit in a different form, in the shallow rural parts of the region. What is involved is translating the folk categories found in the case materials into analytic categories that can be used to understand pattern and variation in rural agrarian economies, not only in Appalachia but in other parts of the world as well.

## A FRAMEWORK FOR UNDERSTANDING SMALL-SCALE RURAL AGRARIAN ECONOMIES

An anthropologist and ethnographer of Appalachia who grew up in the rural South has written, quite poignantly, of his reluctance to consider employing a specialist—plumber, electrician, mason—to perform particular tasks. Why is he so reluctant? To employ a specialist in the culture of rural society is to admit failure and, in part, to deny the accepted division of labor. What kind of failure is involved? The failure is one of coping, that is, how to adapt and to survive by having many different skills (Hicks 1976:4).

Appalachian rural economies, like small-scale rural agrarian economies all over the world, involve multiple activities associated with the following features:

1. A labor-intensive technology of small-scale subsistence food production, known by the folk as "gardening."
2. An almost equally labor-intensive technology of food processing for storage and future consumption, known by the folk as "freezing," "canning," or "putting up" food.
3. The carefully timed use of seasonally variable protein resources including fish, small animals and birds (squirrels, rabbits, quail), and nuts. The folk know these activities as hunting, fishing, and gathering.
4. The availability of a market for cash crops.

5. The availability of internal (within the county) and external wage labor.
6. Reciprocal cooperative labor within the three-generation extended family.

The rich and seasonally variable ecology of the Appalachian region has been well described in the literature. As a whole, the region is extremely rich from an ecological standpoint. This richness permits many varieties of species of flora and fauna to survive and flourish. Such variety contributes to the possibilities for multiple livelihood strategies and multiple sources of income at different times of the year.

Robert Coles has emphasized both the material and the symbolic importance of the land. Symbolically it is home, a theme to which we shall return. Materially it is full of plants, animals, fish, and birds. These are multiple sources of protein and calories. One of Coles' subjects had the following to say about the importance of fish and fishing: "I need worms for fishing. That's what I do when I have time; and we need those fish. My wife some of the time says that if it wasn't for the fish I catch, we'd all be gone by now" (1971:21).

Hunting has been and remains extremely important in rural Appalachian economies. In an early ethnography (1959), Pearsall reports that while hunting no longer constitutes a major economic pursuit, all men and many boys possess shotguns or rifles (1959:46–47). A man rarely leaves the house without his gun, and hunting has only recently declined as the major source of meat. In Brick County, rabbits, squirrels, and deer are still important sources of meat. Meat is dried and cured for long-term use. Hicks also states that hunting and fishing are important sources of protein (1976:28).

The importance of domesticated foods that are produced in gardens cannot be overemphasized in rural agrarian economies, and the Appalachian region is no exception. Gardening is a source of subsistence as well as a source of cash. Early crops such as peas, potatoes, and lettuce are planted in the very early spring and are either consumed directly or "put up" (canned or frozen) for later use. Hicks reports that vegetable gardens are still an important resource for almost all households and people generally expect that families will annually plant, tend, harvest, and preserve a variety of vegetables and fruits for the winter (1976:9). Even the wealthiest families in rural areas, Brick County, and throughout Appalachia plant large gardens. In Plainville the doctor and the produce man both raise large gardens and keep hogs and cows (West 1945:40). Both women and men plant the gardens and weed them. Women prepare (process) the garden products for immediate use and for storage.

In Beech Creek, while gardens and truck patches occupied only small portions of the land under cultivation, most of the food produced and used by the family came from these patches (Schwarzweller, Brown, and Mangalem 1971:6). Ron Eller calls these kitchen gardens the mainstay of the food supply and says that mountain gardens were often quite large. Corn is planted not for sale but for use as feed for hogs, cattle, and chickens (Eller 1982:18–19). We can see that Ruth and Bob, the elderly couple from Brick County, are not atypical. In fact, they may be more typical of the deep rural parts of Appalachia as a whole than has commonly been recognized.

The animals in turn provide milk and meat for home consumption or for trading and selling. One woman aged 59 in Plainville is described by West as a spinster who lives from her garden and $6 monthly rent. "She wants for nothing necessary" (West 1945:41). The staple meat is "hog-meat," which is home butchered and cured in early winter. Three to six large hogs a year are consumed by a family (West 1945:43). Such a pattern is common in Brick County and in other deep rural parts of eastern Kentucky.

As we can see in the life histories of Hattie Kimball and Beatrice Flannery, the seasonality of farm and garden work makes timing of particular kinds of work extremely critical. When the beans were ready, they had to be picked, then processed ("put up") for storage. In Beech Creek, when hogs were killed in the late fall and early winter, women worked very hard in making sausage, butchering, curing meat, and then preparing it for storage (Schwarzweller, Brown, and Mangalem 1971:17). Thus, we can see that the pacing of work, as well as the timing of particular tasks, varies with the seasons. If women in Beech Creek were to work throughout the year at the pace that they work in the fall, they would quickly "burn out."

To summarize this section, one can say that gardening is a pan-Appalachian pattern, with its own intricacies and variations, depending upon which particular region of Appalachia is being considered. It is important to keep in mind that gardening is only one, albeit an important, facet of the multiple livelihood strategy in the deep rural segment. It is combined with wage labor, odd jobs, and cash cropping. The performance of odd jobs, or "hacking around," often carries a pejorative connotation in urban sectors of American culture. But these jobs constitute an important aspect of the overall survival strategy in deep rural Appalachia.

In Brick County, burley tobacco has been the major cash crop. People were never, and are not today, dependent upon cash cropping as their sole, or even their major, source of livelihood. I should note here that the Appalachian literature has devoted relatively little attention to areas in which tobacco is produced (Van Willigen 1989), the assumption being that they are as destitute as the mining towns. In fact, conditions are very different (Hicks 1976:7).

# SIX

# Multiple Livelihood Strategies in the Shallow Rural Area

*Miles was the oldest of us children. He detested farming and barely toler-ated his chores. Daddy knew it and they clashed often. When they were at it, the rest of us knew to be silent.*

*Miles hated to hunt, was uncomfortable with guns even though he was a fairly good shot. He didn't mind killing things so much, but would rather be curled up with a book. Daddy would make him go anyway, and if he came back empty handed, would berate him before us all at the dinner table. I longed to go hunting, but Daddy only laughed when I mentioned it.*

*"Ain't fitting for a girl," he'd say.*

*Giardina (1987:34)*

Heading south from Columbus and Cincinnati or north from Lexington, one encounters a land of contrasts, even anomalies. Barns with live-stock grazing in the foreground; factories covering the horizon in the background. Signs in cornfields that say, "Let Toyota be your neighbor." Shopping malls rear up in the midst of mobile home parks. Barns with tobacco drying from the rafters can be seen from the road just before a colorful billboard invites visitors to a large flea market. The major inter-state highway passes an industrial park that looks as though a strong wind might easily demolish the flimsy buildings. This is the area of the shallow rural. There are many such areas in the United States and, in-deed, in the world. This is the area in between the urban and the deep rural. Here subsistence and cash economies overlap in subtle ways. The intertwining of work tasks in several economic sectors is not really ap-parent. The case history that follows, that of Chip, shows some of the complex combinations of livelihood strategies in several different kinds of economies.

## CHIP

Chip lives in a mobile home settlement in the center of the shallow rural. The settlement is a pleasant place located just off a country road. The homes are on good-sized plots of land that are big enough for small gardens. Many people have attached shaded porches to their mobile homes. Chip has enough room in his yard to fix farm machinery and to store his tools. He works for a construction company that is based in the shallow rural area; he does sandblasting and bricklaying. Although he has been with the same construction firm for 29 years, the availability of work for him is always unstable. As a result, Chip has always managed to maintain other sources of cash. In the winter of 1986, when business was slow, Chip took a voluntary lay-off.

Throughout much of his adult life, Chip has used the regional marketplace system as both a buyer and a seller. He shops at the large Redside Market each weekend for groceries for his household and for tools that he can recondition for resale. He and a friend also frequent a weekly auction where they look for good used tools.

To supplement his cash income, for the last seven years Chip has sold slab bark that he buys from a company in the eastern part of the state. The wood is too uneven to be of use to the lumber company but sells well as firewood. He arranges many of the sales of wood during the time he spends in the marketplaces. In 1986 he generated nearly $16,000 from wood sales alone. His reputation spreads by word of mouth, and his slab bark business is growing. Chip has reinvested a large part of his earnings into his operation and has fixed up his truck so that he can carry more wood from the lumberyard.

This chapter, designed to introduce the reader to the area I call the shallow rural, is intended to provide a sense of the context within which multiple livelihood strategies operate, specifically the context within which marketplaces and places of wage labor employment occur. A large portion of this chapter describes the multiple livelihood strategies used by five extended families who reside in a hamlet in the shallow rural area (see Figure 1). Why do we use the term shallow rural? Why is it a focal point of the analysis?

## SHALLOW RURAL AS A MODEL

The model of the shallow rural is designed to describe and analyze a segment of the region for which there is no folk term. Like the model of the deep rural, the model of the shallow rural also has geographical, ecological, and cultural designations. What are its core features? The model emphasizes the essentially rural nature of the area. Gardens and farms

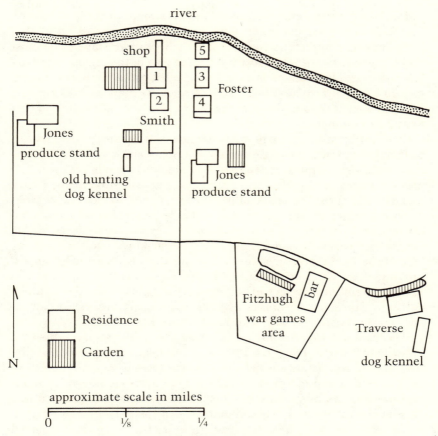

river

shop

Foster

Smith

Jones

produce stand

old hunting
dog kennel

Jones

produce stand

Fitzhugh

war games
area

bar

Traverse

dog kennel

N

☐ Residence

▥ Garden

approximate scale in miles

0    ⅛    ¼

*Figure 1. A sketch map of a shallow rural hamlet*

are prominent on the landscape. The term *shallow* is meant to indicate the area's geographical accessibility to the city and its tenuousness as a rural area. Its accessibility to both country and city is accomplished primarily through a complex and substantial infrastructure, in this case a system of interstate highways. Since factories and marketplaces are located in the shallow rural, but not in the deep rural areas, people can gain relatively easy access to jobs in the capitalist wage labor sector and to cash from marketplace sales. Shopping malls can be found in shallow, but not in deep rural areas, and they provide people access to the products of the capitalist economy. Thus, the shallow rural is geographically close to the urban areas, yet its resource base still allows for agrarian production. Shallow rural contrasts with deep rural, but is also related to it. The deep rural areas are much less accessible to the city because they lack the infrastructure.

As indicated in the introduction, the shallow rural is by far the most problematic as well as the most interesting part of the region. Not only is it a gray area between country and city, but it contains the most intricate and changing mix of livelihood strategies. Its rural features are fragile; they are endangered daily by the forces of industrialization and economic development.

The shallow rural is also problematic precisely because, to my knowledge, it has not been a category in social science analysis. Usually areas such as this are simply referred to as rural. In order to indicate the differences between two qualitatively different, but still rural areas, I have divided rural into deep and shallow. As I have mentioned, that there is no folk category for this part of the region is indicative of its problematic features. Taking clues from the folk categories, the "in-between" status of this area became more and more striking. The fact that the core of the marketplace system is found in the shallow rural is important and highlights certain characteristics of this area. Deep rural and urban economies intersect in the marketplaces, as do rural and urban cultures. The shallow rural is distinctive precisely because it can accommodate the mix of economies and cultures.

The shallow rural surrounds a major interstate highway; it is also the location of Fenwick Industrial Park, which is itself a temporary installation in that its existence is based on the tax incentives the city of Fenwick has offered to industry. The majority of firms are housed in semipermanent aluminum buildings that were quickly prefabricated and built in the early 1970s. These buildings can easily be evacuated, torn down, and removed when the firms are forced to leave the industrial park. When the tax legislation expires, the park is expected to close. The park is situated in the center of the region, close to the major interstate highway. The park covers approximately five square miles and houses 30 separate firms. Most of the companies are manufacturing operations or warehouse facilities. They range from full-scale heavy industry to storage and distribution centers. The introduction of the industrial park to the area has caused many changes in the surrounding area. The need for housing and service-oriented businesses, created by the increase of workers, has quickened the development of Fenwick, although the town still had a population of only 15,000 in 1988.

What was once farmland has been turned into residential developments. Many apartment buildings, condominiums, and tract housing developments have appeared since the opening of the industrial park. One farmer in the vicinity has resisted the move toward such development by refusing to leave his farm. In the midst of apartment buildings and fast food restaurants, there still stands one farmstead. The owner is an elderly farmer who refuses to give up his land even in the face of a lawsuit. Aside from this one holdout, the immediate area of the industrial park has recently filled with migrants in search of wage labor jobs. This wave of migration is evident in the county population statistics that show a 13.2 percent increase in the last 10 years. Temporary workers in the industrial park constantly talk about how happy they are to have the knowledge and skills necessary to maintain a garden large enough to feed a family for an extended period. People brag about how they could "make do" in the event of an "economic crunch." They talk about the farming life-style as "the best," "the most natural," and "the salt of the earth way to live." While the majority of workers in the park live in or near the shallow rural, there are those who choose to commute from the deep rural. One informant told us of several people who commute to the industrial park either daily or weekly from other parts of the state and region. Examples of people driving distances of 100 miles or more are not uncommon.

## A SHALLOW RURAL HAMLET

This section describes the multiple livelihood strategies used by five extended families living in a hamlet located in the shallow rural area of the region. It provides a picture of the residential context from which people operate their multiple livelihood strategies. The hamlet represents a microcosm of the regional pattern of multiple livelihood strategies. People who live in the hamlet have kin who live nearby in other hamlets in the shallow rural area. They also have kin ties in the deep rural area and in the city as well.

The hamlet is located near the town of Shallow Creek, Kentucky, in Cantor County, approximately eight miles south of a major city in the region. The town was founded in 1841 and had a population of 2,200 in 1987 (1980 census). The area of the town is approximately two square miles, broken down as follows: 50 percent residential, 10 percent industrial or manufacturing, 10 percent commercial, and 30 percent developable. This last statistic is interesting because the 30 percent is essentially farmland. The town is the home of eight churches: five churches are of Fundamentalist denominations; one is Roman Catholic; one, Lutheran; and one, Episcopal. Membership in a church reflects the town's stratification pattern. Most people in the town, including working-class people, belong to one of the Fundamentalist churches, the most common type of church found in the deep rural. With a few exceptions, virtually all of the people in this study belonged to Fundamentalist churches. Most of the Roman Catholics are of German descent and represent, for the most part, the elite of the region.

The hamlet is not named. The average homestead in the hamlet occupies at least one acre of land, with subsistence garden plots tended by family members. The composition of the homesteads is varied. In one case the entire extended family can be found in a cluster of households on the homestead. In most other cases, however, people in the hamlet have kin living in the region. Some family members live in the same mobile home park as Chip, which is a 10- or 15-minute drive from the hamlet. Others live in the same county, and still others live in the deep rural areas. Virtually everyone in the hamlet raises fruits, vegetables, and other farm products for their own consumption by putting considerable amounts of effort and planning into their subsistence gardens. When necessary, they recruit the labor of family members from throughout the region to help with all stages of garden work, from clearing and planting, to weeding and harvesting, to processing for storage and consumption. Selling goods in the periodic marketplace system, which we describe and analyze in the next two chapters, is an important activity for many of the people who live in the hamlet. The marketplaces are sources of necessary cash. Most of the adults have had some experience in the wage labor sector as well. There are also other means of generating cash in the hamlet. Small, self-owned or family-owned businesses generate cash for three of the families in the hamlet. These businesses also employ family and hamlet members. Many of the men in the hamlet perform odd jobs, or handywork, both within and outside of the town and the hamlet. Beyond these work tasks, the people in the hamlet are linked to one another by ties of trading and mutual assistance. Home-canned produce, vegetables, and used household items move around the hamlet according to need. People from the hamlet also buy goods in the marketplaces, since the prices are substantially lower than prices in nearby supermarkets and shopping malls.

## THE FOSTER FAMILY

The Foster family homestead consists of five houses in which a total of 29 people reside. Three generations can be found in the five households, including distant cousins. The family did not always live in this concentrated arrangement. They came to the town of Shallow Creek after the steel mills in Neville began to lay off workers. As noted in chapter 4, the layoffs were associated with strikes that began in the 1920s and have continued up to the present. Several male family members lost their jobs, and the Fosters shifted their sources of livelihood away from the wage labor sector.[1]

Four generations are present in this largest household: Grandmother and Grandfather Foster, their son and his wife, a grandson and his wife and young son. Directly across the street lives a married daughter, her husband, and two children. To the south of the main Foster house live three generations of cousins: a married couple, their son and his wife and two children, a boy and a girl. To the north of the daughter's home is the home of more distantly related cousins: a married couple and their two daughters and one son. To the south of the daughter's home is another group of Foster cousins, three generations including grandparents, their married son and his wife and two sons.

Grandmother and Grandfather Foster were raised in the deep rural part of the region and act as organizers for the homestead. It should be noted here that the Foster family could easily fit into Arensberg's book *The Irish Countryman* in which the power of the grandparents, particularly the grandfather, is described in great detail for three-generation extended families. Both of the Foster grandparents have played an important part in raising their grandchildren and now great-grandchildren. A neighbor from across the street comments that Grandfather Foster can be seen playing with the "little ones" and teaching them basic skills such as how to drive a nail. Grandfather Foster also has a reputation as a storyteller and yarnspinner and can often be found relating stories about his work experiences in the factories or his farm work in the deep rural part of the region. The large front porch of his house is the gathering place for the entire extended family. Used Greyhound Bus seats rest on the porch and provide ample seating.

A small welding shop abuts the main Foster house. It is operated by the older males in the Foster household, who do many of the small welding jobs in the local area. As often as once a month, the extended Foster family will organize a large yard sale on the front lawn of the main house. Used household goods from many "branches" of the kin network are sold, along with some produce, depending on the season. Frequently, other households in the hamlet join in these sales by providing used goods and family labor. The result is the generation of cash for those who contribute goods and labor to the sale.

The extended Foster family furnishes most of its own foodstuffs in a self-sufficient manner. A subsistence garden in the back of the main Foster house provides produce for the extended family, as well as some produce for sale in the family yard sales. The produce that is not immediately consumed by the family or sold for cash is canned and stored for winter use. Grandmother Foster organizes the work necessary for canning and storing—a not inconsiderable amount of labor. Some of the protein requirements of the extended family are met by the hogs raised by Grandfather Foster on a small lot behind the main house. There are facilities for butchering the hogs on the premises, and the family, along with some neighbors, is provided with pork for the entire year. On rare occasions meat will be butchered for people outside the hamlet for a small fee. The pork the Fosters raise is also traded around the neighborhood network in exchange for a variety of goods and services.

Members of the Foster family are involved in a mix of permanent and temporary wage labor employments. Almost all of the members of the family have participated in temporary wage labor at some point. The son of the cousins to the north of the daughter's house has just come of age to enter the temporary labor system. He uses his income to rent the apartment adjacent to his family's home, thus providing them with cash. Previously, this apartment had been rented by a waitress who was not a member of the family. It is not uncommon for kin to engage in renting, buying, and selling arrangements with one another (Bryant 1981). However, we do not know whether the Foster cousin paid a lower rent by virtue of his kinship ties. The Foster family, well-known in the neighborhood, is admired for their cohesive family group and their hardworking attitude.

## THE SMITH FAMILY

The Smith house is located to the south of the Foster homestead on the main road running through the hamlet. Harry and Ilene Smith are in their sixties. They have one daughter, who is married and lives in the mobile home park about six miles away from the hamlet. The Smiths also engage in a number of strategies for making ends meet, but since they have a smaller family and are both retired, the composition of the multiple strategies is very different from that of the Foster family. Harry's case history illustrates multiple strategies and differential use of the subsistence and cash-generating sectors over time.

Harry was born in 1920 and grew up on the family farm in Brick County. There the Smith family farm consisted of 300 acres of land with between 300 and 400 head of sheep. It was primarily a self-sustaining subsistence farm with a large garden. The family sold the wool from the sheep, a strategy that reflects the family's Scottish ancestry dating back to the nineteenth century. Harry's siblings were a sister named Emerald, 10 years younger than he, and a brother who died at the age of 21 of a "burst" appendix. Emerald is an extraordinarily vigorous woman who lives in the region. She works with her husband, who owns a garage, and spends most of her working time driving a truck to bring spare auto parts to the garage. She has just bought a new house by the river, with good bottomland which benefits from the fertilizer and soil washed down from higher ground. She maintains a large garden.

In 1940 Harry married Ilene Rowan, who was also from Brick County. Ilene was born in 1919, one of seven children. Ilene's parents were tenant tobacco farmers. Her paternal uncle, Kale, lived with the family. Everyone worked in the tobacco fields. Ilene was known as an extremely organized and energetic person. From the time she was seven, she worked consistently in the household, cleaning, straightening, and caring for small children. At the age of nine, Ilene began raising turkeys for cash. She used the cash to buy bolts of cloth for dresses. Her entrepreneurial endeavor stemmed from the fact that her father typically picked out her clothes. She says she knew he was thinking ahead and trying to provide for his family, but she was tired of wearing dark colors that would hide dirt and wear. She also disliked clothing that was three times her size, a future-oriented provision to allow for her growth. Ilene loved school and learning and excelled in her studies. Her father, however, believed that an eighth-grade education was enough for anyone. High school was play, and college was nonsense. The principal of the Brick County school system recognized Ilene's potential and her father's stubbornness, so he came to the Rowan farm in person to try to convince Ilene's father to allow her to attend high school. Her father refused and asked the principal to leave the farm. Ilene confesses to crying after this incident, but she says, "It didn't help matters, and so I went back to my farm chores."

During her childhood, Ilene trapped rabbits with her male siblings and sold them to a huckster. She was an excellent shot but would not hunt because she enjoyed watching wildlife, especially birds. "Besides," she said, "the boys kept plenty of meat on the table. . . . why waste?" Ilene has always loved fishing. In her days on the family farm, to afford a fishing pole was unheard of. "Some thread and a safety pin did just fine." Berrying and hunting for greens were her favorite food-gathering activities. She loved to go out with her uncle because he knew a great deal about wildlife.

In Brick County, Harry and Ilene grew up together. They attended the same school and the same church; they were always friends and began courting in their teen years. Upon their marriage in 1940, Harry and Ilene left Brick County and came to "town" in the shallow rural. They chose to live in Neville because the Yellow Stripe busline to Brick County ran right through the center of town.

In his early years in Cantor County, Harry walked from Neville across the Ohio River to New City, Ohio, where he worked for the Coca Cola Company. He held this job for 17 years, driving and delivering. At

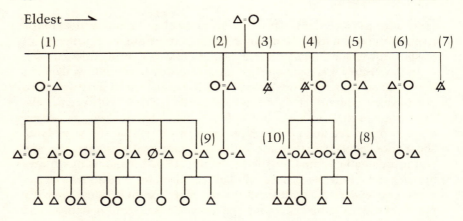

*Figure 2. Irene Smith's family network*

first Ilene worked for a florist in a shallow rural town in Kentucky. She later took a streetcar to the city to be a receptionist in a dentist's office, where she worked until 1981. Every Friday afternoon for many years, Harry and Ilene went home to Brick County. They alternated visiting his parents and hers, along with other relatives.

Ilene's family network is quite extensive (see Figure 2). Her sister, Linda Marks (5), is employed at a crafts supply store. She also has a craft business at home and produces paintings, ceramics, wreaths, refrigerator magnets, and other crafts. Linda can purchase craft items that are reduced for sale at her place of employment and also uses her employee discount to purchase goods. Linda's husband, Dan (5), works for Coca Cola and also fishes, hunts, and saws firewood. Dan contributes to yard sales and to craft manufacture because he is skilled with various saws and is able to cut out wooden figures for the women to paint. Ilene's husband, Harry, secured the job for Dan at Coca Cola, and because Dan has worked there since 1950, he has a substantial income. He uses his money to purchase materials and tools that Harry cannot afford. However, when there is a large project to tackle, such as major auto repair or roofing, Dan seeks out Harry for his depth of experience. Dan and Linda frequently travel to the deep rural areas on fishing expeditions. Since Harry and Ilene are getting older, they are not as able to travel this distance. Dan and Linda always share their catch with Ilene and Harry. They usually bring back several coolers of fish prepared for the freezer.

Linda's daughter, Sally, is employed at the Goody Company in Cincinnati and regularly takes crafts produced by her mother to sell at work. Sally and her husband, David, live in a small town in Cantor County. He is a construction worker, which means that he is employed seasonally. When he is not working on a construction job, he is an avid outdoorsman, and their freezer is virtually always full of meat and fish from his expeditions. David recently began raising hunting dogs for sale. The employees of the Goody Company, especially those in management positions, will often commission Linda to make special items such as flower arrangements for them. At the same time that Linda started her business, Lou Ann Rist (6), Ilene's sister-in-law, began a retail business in a well-to-do town in the shallow rural. Her husband, Wally, is also a seasonal construction worker. During his off season, he is very active in hunting and fishing. Lou Ann commissions Linda to make crafts for her shop. Ilene also makes pillows, bittersweet wreaths, and flower arrangements to sell in Lou Ann's shop. Linda herself exchanges her crafts with Ilene for fresh garden produce, when in season. Ilene then takes many of the craft items to the marketplaces to sell. It is important to note, however, that pillows that would normally sell in the marketplaces for $10 to $12 will sell in Lou Ann's shop for $25 each. The shop cleared $50,000 in 1987. Items that do not sell in the shop or in the marketplaces are sent to another sister-in-law of Ilene's, Mary Rowan (4), who lives in a town in the shallow rural near a historic town that draws many tourists. She normally sells her wares in yard sales. The profits she derives from her sales are used to purchase antique furniture from local estate sales. She refinishes the furniture and sells it to tourists who visit the historic town.

Harry has worked at many different tasks throughout his life, some simultaneously. After his employment at Coca-Cola, his wage labor jobs included working a water station in Cantor County and stripping furniture for a man in Neville. In addition, he painted houses, repaired typewriters, and raised bird dogs for sale. These were beagles that were used for hunting rabbits, squirrels, and quail.

Harry has passed on his skills as an outdoorsman to his nephew Mark. Since Mark's father, husband of Harry's sister, was a small businessman who, with the exception of his riverbottom garden, has little interest in the outdoors, Harry always made sure that he included Mark in his hunting and fishing endeavors. Because Harry visited his sister's homestead quite often, Mark developed a very close relationship to Harry. Mark's son, now age eight, is already a rather accomplished marksman and regularly accompanies Mark on deer-hunting expeditions. Mark, in turn, provides Harry's daughter and son-in-law with large quantities (30 pounds in the summer of 1987) of venison in the form of hamburger, steaks, and roasts.

Throughout their adulthood, Harry and Ilene raised a large garden and, until recently, kept an orchard of pear, plum, peach, cherry, and

## TABLE 3
## Monthly Family Budget: Ilene and Harry

| | |
|---|---:|
| **Monthly income:** | |
| Social Security—Ilene | $ 200 |
| Social Security—Harry | 150 |
| Veteran's pension—Harry | 300 |
| Yard sales/gun trade (minimal estimate) | 200 |
| | $ 850 |
| | |
| **Monthly expenditures:** | |
| Electricity/gas | $ 50 |
| Water | 30 |
| Sanitation | 20 |
| Phone | 25 |
| Grocery (garden savings!) | 100 |
| Gasoline | 40 |
| | $ 265 |
| | |
| **Yearly expenditures:** | |
| Taxes per year | $ 200 |
| Health insurance | 1,200 |
| Car insurance | 500 |
| Home insurance | 400 |
| Income tax | 0 |
| | $2,300 |

apple trees. They also grew grapes. The fruit was used for their own consumption; much of it was put up for the winter; and about half of it was
sold as fresh produce (see Table 3).

In 1970 Harry and Ilene moved to their current (smaller) homestead.
They gave up the orchard but still maintain a garden. Six years ago they
began growing large quantities of tomatoes on a regular basis, selling
enough tomatoes to a local restaurant to buy sugar to put up wild
raspberries and blackberries for jam for the winter. Harry has continued
to paint both the interiors and the exteriors of houses. Harry and Ilene
also sell as regular vendors in the marketplace system. Their activities
are described in chapter 5.

In 1984–1985 Harry underwent open heart surgery. As a veteran, he
received first-rate health care in a combination of VA hospitals in Cin-

cinnati and Cleveland. He and his family experienced great anxiety, however, when they tried to extract information from the hospital's house staff (residents and interns) and from the attending physician. As rural people in an urban Veterans Administration hospital, they were given perfunctory answers to their questions about Harry's prognosis and were treated with some rudeness by the nursing staff. When they asked to talk to Harry's doctor, they were forced to wait several days before the physician returned Ilene's telephone call. When Harry was sent to Cleveland, where the open heart surgery was performed, he was extremely lonely. As he was being taken off the plane on his return to Cincinnati, his daughter told me that he "cried like a baby, he was so happy to be home." Three weeks after the surgery, Harry was out shooting squirrels. Before the surgery, Harry worked as a handyman for several people. In the last several months, he has reactivated some of his relationships with his customers and has begun to perform odd jobs with his son-in-law, Nathan, a carpenter who had also held several jobs as a temporary wage laborer.

## THE JONES FAMILY

Alfred and his wife, another couple in their sixties, live on the north side of the main road to the east of the Smith house. Alfred is retired from a job as a milk inspector after 30 years with a single company. The couple recently moved to the hamlet from a home in the northern part of the region; the home was destroyed to make way for an interstate highway. The couple has several children living nearby in a town similar to Shallow Creek.

During the summer months, Alfred constructs a fruit and vegetable stand in front of his house. His own garden produce, and occasionally the produce of his neighbors, brings him enough cash for groceries. Alfred has been selling produce for a number of years; before his retirement Alfred spent weekends operating a fruit and vegetable stand on a major local highway for 27 years. His new location is profitable though, especially when the Foster family yard sales bring significant numbers of buyers into the hamlet. He also has a regular regional clientele who know him for his prizes at the county fair.

Alfred inherited a farm in Alexandria, a nearby town in the shallow rural area, from his parents, and the bulk of his produce comes from there. Every day, in season, he takes his truck to the farm and picks corn, tomatoes, zucchini, several kinds of beans and peppers, cabbage, broccoli, eggplant, and okra.

Alfred and his wife frequently use the local flea markets as sources of manufactured goods such as household items and supplies for gardening.

## THE TRAVERSE FAMILY

The Traverse family house sits in the far eastern part of the hamlet, about three miles east of the Smith place. Biff and Henrietta Traverse live in the house with their five children, three daughters and two sons. Biff has a wage labor position in a local factory, and Henrietta and the two eldest daughters hold jobs in a large hotel in the city. Henrietta works as a middle manager, and her daughters are receptionists. Biff works as a carpenter "on the side."

In addition to their employment in the wage sector, the family maintains a large subsistence garden. Biff also raises bird dogs for sale as a means of generating extra cash. The family owns a large farm south of the hamlet. Biff visits the farm nearly every weekend and takes his sons and some neighborhood children along to help him with the farm work. Biff has commented that he would like very much to move to the farm on a full-time basis. His sons agree. Henrietta and her daughters are very much opposed to this move and would prefer, if any move is taken by the family, to move toward the city so that they can be close to the hotel where they are employed. At this point, the home in the hamlet is a compromise. There is tension in this family between country and city. Males and females align themselves on rural and urban axes, respectively. In 1989 I learned of Biff's and Henrietta's divorce. She and her daughters moved to the city. He went back to his farm.

## THE FITZHUGH FAMILY

Across the wooded area that lies to the south of the Thompson land is the Fitzhugh homestead. The Fitzhughs are a large extended family comprised of anywhere from 21 to 26 members at any given time. The family spans four generations. The Fitzhugh homestead is nearly self-sufficient because it can rely on several small, family-owned businesses and a large subsistence garden.

Approximately seven years ago, the family opened a recreational area to the public. The space was used to admit people to play a war-type survival game that requires several acres of land. The game is open year-round and attracts hundreds of people each week. The family operates a booth at an annual local fair just for the purpose of advertising the game. The popularity and consequent economic success of the recreation area provided the Fitzhugh family with the incentive to open another business. Adjacent to the front of the Fitzhugh house is a small bar. It has been in operation for about six years. Family members staff both of the small businesses and supply the household with a substantial amount of cash. Some family members take on odd jobs as well.

## SUMMARY

We can see from these cases that family networks operate by using a series of multiple livelihood strategies. These strategies are geared toward the maintenance of the people in the network. The strategies vary, depending upon the size and composition of the network and the life course position of its members. All people in the hamlet have access to the resources of both the country and the city, although some deal with the country and its resources more extensively and more regularly than others who work primarily in the city. There is a considerable amount of variability in the hamlet regarding the size and the location of family networks. In the case of the Foster family, the entire family network can be found living in the hamlet. Their residence pattern is, in fact, closer to that of the deep rural, in which families live side by side on homesteads and in communities. The Foster family is remarkably self-sustaining, as are the other families in the hamlet. For the other families, however, segments of the family network actually reside in the hamlet, and others are dispersed throughout the region.

The fact that people from the deep rural areas hold property in the shallow rural is extremely important because the same sense of autonomy and control that owning property conferred in the deep rural is replicated in the shallow rural. People talk about the foolishness of giving up land and the knowledge of how to work it. Children are encouraged to live in places with "at least some land." A mobile home is preferable to an apartment complex because a small garden is possible. Without land, older people lament the loss of control of some part of their livelihood; this is true even when their children "are working good jobs." The possession of land allows people to opt out of the market economy at will. More important, land and family ties provide people with a sense of control over their lives. Maintaining one's place in the family network is essential for maintaining that control. The family histories show that no single person or family is dependent on one source of livelihood—neither a single source of cash nor a single means of subsistence. Also, no single age-group is responsible for providing the livelihood of families. All members of the family's households, whether or not they are coresidential households, contribute to the maintenance of the family network.

All of the people in the shallow rural hamlet who are over the age of 40 grew up on family farms in the deep rural parts of the region. In the deep rural, subsistence farming was always combined with various cash-generating strategies, including the cash cropping of tobacco and soybeans, livestock raising, truck gardening, and off-farm wage labor. Hunting wild game (rabbits, squirrel, quail, deer), along with fishing and the gathering of wild fruits and nuts, transfers from the deep to the shallow rural. Much flexibility can be found in the system of multiple livelihood strategies. When one source of livelihood slackens or fails altogether, as was the case in the closing of the steel mill, people create other sources of livelihood on a rural base. The people in the shallow rural hamlet are aware that "not putting all your eggs in one basket" is the most reliable and secure approach to livelihood. That multiple strategies require the cooperation and coordination of family networks is well recognized by the folk.

# SEVEN

# The Structure of a Regional Marketplace System (with Sara Sturdevant)

*The large number of markets might seem at first sight to contradict the commercial paralysis of the age, for from the beginning of the ninth century they increased rapidly and new ones were continually being founded. But their number is itself proof of their insignificance. Only the fair of St. Denys, near Paris, attracted once a year, among its pilgrims, occasional sellers and buyers from a distance. Apart from it there were only innumerable small weekly markets, where the peasants of the district offered for sale a few eggs, chickens, pounds of wool, or ells of coarse cloth woven at home.*

*(Pirenne 1937)*

*Most of the traders at the stockyard are farmers who trade in secondhand goods on the side. Cleo is shocked to realize this, though she knows nobody can make a living on a farm these days. She recognizes some of the farmers, behind their folding tables of dusty old objects. Even at the time of Jake's death, feeding the cows was costing as much as the milk brought. She cannot imagine Jake in a camper, peddling old junk from the barn. That would kill him if the heart attack hadn't.*

*Cleo and Rita Jean drift from table to table, touching Depression glass, crystal goblets, cracked china, cast-off egg beaters and mixers, rusted farm implements, and greasy wooden boxes stuffed with buttons and papers.*

*"I never saw so much old stuff," says Cleo.*

*"Look at this," says Rita Jean, pointing to a box of plastic jump ropes. "These aren't old."*

*Mason (1982:91)*

Bringing goods to marketplaces to trade and to sell dates back to ancient times. The Greek *agora*, the Middle Eastern bazaar, the solar markets of

Mesoamerica, the weekly markets of the Caribbean, and the Javanese *pasar* are only a few examples. Craft items, agricultural products, and more recently, manufactured goods can be found arrayed in marketplaces all over the world. Marketplaces are ordinarily associated with the Third World, as links between rural subsistence economies and as arenas for generating small amounts of cash. They have not been dealt with as a reaction to or a consequence of deindustrialization or as a response to a shrinking cash crop sector.

Marketplaces in this part of the Appalachian region share many features with marketplaces throughout the world (Beals 1970, 1975, 1976; Belshaw 1965; Calnek 1978; Chapman 1957; Cook 1976; Cook and Diskin 1976; Diskin 1969, 1976; Geertz 1963, 1979; Hill 1966; D. Kaplan 1965; Malinowski and de la Fuente 1957; Marroquin 1957; Ortiz 1967; Plattner 1985, 1989; Skinner 1964). Understanding the structure of the periodic marketing system is necessary for understanding how marketing activities contribute to the overall pattern of multiple livelihood strategies. This chapter sets out the basic structure of the marketplace system. Chapter 8 contains case histories of sellers who use the marketplace system differentially. By examining the different combinations of strategies used by members of family networks, we can begin to understand the factors that contribute to the persistence of multiple livelihood strategies. The purpose of this chapter is to present a picture of the system of periodic marketplaces so that the relative importance of marketplace activities in relationship to the complex of livelihood strategies in a regional context can be understood.

Marketplaces are public, open spaces, indoor and outdoor, or a combination of the two, to which people bring goods to sell and trade. The goods come from many different sources: farms and gardens, factories, and auctions. New and used goods, trinkets, and old farm tools can be seen in great abundance along with produce (wholesale and home-grown), crafts, and a myriad of other items. The folk call these "flea markets." Urbanites might view the markets as quaint and even idiosyncratic sources of diversion or as the places to find bargains in antiques.

The marketplaces are part of an organized system that has a definite structure, with definite rules, sanctions, and opportunities. They are major arenas for generating cash by selling goods and also provide opportunities for people to barter goods for other goods. The marketplaces distribute goods to people in the region as well. For some people, marketing activities occupy great amounts of time, perhaps the equivalent of a full-time job. For most people, however, marketing represents one piece of a multifaceted livelihood strategy. Many booths in marketplaces appear to function like small family businesses without the overhead costs and without the tax encumbrances. As we have seen from the histories of people in Shallow Creek, the family network is the economic unit. In every family at least one member, and usually two or more, is involved in marketplace activities. In many instances the entire family network regularly attends the markets.

Selling in marketplaces is a major way of generating the cash needed to buy items that people do not produce themselves. As one seller in the marketplace put it, marketing provides the money to "feed the farm." As we shall see, complex relationships exist between market selling (distribution) and agrarian production (farming and gardening). Sellers not only sell to customers, for whom the low prices are essential but also sell to and trade with one another in a manner that mirrors patterns of trading in other parts of the rural United States (West 1945). Buying and trading in marketplaces have become critical to consumption patterns in the northeastern Kentucky region, especially for people in the shallow rural.

Marketing activities take place in a system of marketplaces. The system can be described as a classic rural periodic marketplace system (cf. Skinner 1964) consisting of hierarchically organized markets of different sizes with different schedules of operation. People use markets selectively, depending upon the goods they have to sell. The system affects when and where people set up their booths as well as what kinds of goods they bring to the marketplace. The markets are periodic because different markets meet on different days, regularly, from week to week.

It is rather remarkable to find a marketplace system such as this in the midst of an industrializing area of northeastern Kentucky. Again, it should be emphasized that this is not just an occasional flea market or antique barn; it is a structured system. Why do we find a regional marketplace system in this region? Understood in historical and cultural contexts, one can say that the system has come into being in response to the decline of tobacco as a cash crop. This is certainly true, but there is more to it. Two features of the marketplace structure should be noted and emphasized. The first is that the structure itself is extremely flexible. Since the structure is flexible and changing, people can participate in the marketplaces at different levels of frequency and intensity. As will be seen in the next chapter, people can sell in marketplaces as a full-time activity, or they can use the marketplaces only occasionally such that marketplace activities represent only a small part of their overall livelihood strategy. The flexibility of the marketplace system supports the diversity and lack of specialization that are such important elements of the Kentucky way. Different markets meet on different days, are different sizes, operate in different locations (sometimes changing location in different seasons) and attract different clientele.

The second important feature of the marketplace structure is that the patterns of interaction between sellers, as they move within what is a rather elaborate and complicated system, resemble relationships between neighbors and kin in community contexts. There is a definite feeling of closeness among groups of market sellers. People look in on one another's booths, much as neighbors look in on the elderly and the sick in rural communities. Richard Newhold, one of the first vendors at the Redside Market (a major market) is ill with cancer. On April 30, 1988, several other vendors at the market helped transport Newhold's goods from his booth to his home. Harry Smith said that "the market was like a funeral home." Everyone was very sad and doing all that they could to comfort Mrs. Newhold and their son.

## MARKETPLACES AND MARKET SYSTEMS

It is essential to mention the distinction between a system of marketplaces and a market system (Polanyi, Arensberg, and Pearson 1957). A system of marketplaces is simply a grouping of marketplaces, a grouping that can be located in actual geographical space. A market system, by contrast, is not a physically grounded, geographically based system at all, but rather an abstract structure that consists of mechanisms of supply and demand that determine the price of a given item and, in turn, how much of that item will be produced for "the market." Thus, in a market system there is feedback between distribution and production processes. The price of potatoes will be determined by the actual supply balanced against the actual demand for them. In a system of marketplaces, the price of potatoes may, to some degree be influenced by supply and demand forces, but potatoes and all produce, for that matter, will be valued differently in the marketplace than in the supermarket. Potatoes will commonly be traded among sellers for other items; the terms of the trade may be determined by the relationships between the parties to the trade, or by a number of other factors, including the time of day. Perishable items will become less costly as the day goes on.

Many of the goods sold in the marketplaces were produced originally for the market system. The majority of the new items present in the marketplaces are seconds, irregulars, or overstocks. Vendors attempt to sell items that are not wanted by the larger commercial market. The new items may be obtained through connections that the seller's family members have with production and distribution networks in the region. For example, people who work in the Levi's factory will know when the seconds will be available for sale. Goods may also be obtained from a variety of small businesses, usually operated by the seller or by a family member. Booths in the marketplaces that operate by using the "throwaways" of the market system may offer anything from vitamins and packages of socks to stationery and cosmetics. It is not uncommon to find a booth with boxes of pencils inscribed with the name of a small business firm that is no longer operating; the pencils, originally commissioned by the company, may sell for as little as $.25 per 100. Clothing that is no longer in style or bottled salad dressings whose dates have expired are other examples of goods originally produced for the market system.

Sellers may buy wholesale goods directly from the manufacturing firms. Sales people from various companies may visit the markets in order to find new clients. We saw such a salesman at one of the minor markets; he went from booth to booth promoting what he termed "good dollar items," small goods that can be sold for a dollar. Inexpensive, faddish items such as toys, cosmetics, and jewelry fill many booths. Wholesalers also advertise their goods designated for flea markets in a number of publications. Vendors obtain these publications in the major marketplaces and use them frequently. Many of the wholesale companies are located within the region and are easily accessible to marketplace sellers. New goods may also become available when a seller is closing down a booth. The entire contents of the booth may be purchased by another seller at a reduced price.

Produce is always available at the majority of the markets in the regional system. Major markets offer fruits and vegetables year-round, and the smaller, more seasonal minor markets usually include at least one produce booth. Produce available in the regional system varies seasonally, with sellers obtaining fruit and vegetables in the winter through large-scale wholesalers in the city. The seller who uses these companies must go to the produce warehouses daily, for after wholesalers allocate produce to supermarkets and restaurants, they offer what is left to small-scale buyers at a reduced rate. Also sellers buy fruits and vegetables that are not accepted by larger firms because of blemishes or other imperfections. In the summer, produce sellers usually offer items that they or their families have grown in gardens and on truck farms, setting out green beans or tomatoes alongside used goods. On a slightly larger scale, the Fruit Man, who owns and operates a small farm and winery in rural Ohio in conjunction with his brothers, offers produce from the farm along with other foods, such as nuts and dried fruits, that he buys from a local wholesaler.

## HIERARCHICAL STRUCTURE

The regional periodic marketplace system in this Appalachian region is hierarchically organized in that some markets are larger than others and that more sellers draw more buyers. The system resembles the dendritic system described by Carol Smith (1976a, 1976b) for the regional marketplace system in Guatemala in the sense that the marketplaces are nested. Small or minor markets are associated with intermediate markets. Intermediate markets feed into major markets because people purchase goods in the intermediate markets and sell them in the major markets. Major marketplaces are also centrally located; they are situated directly adjacent to the main interstate highway. Intermediate markets can be found along state and county roads. The smallest, or minor, markets are tucked along local country roads. The structure of the marketplace system permits sellers to use all three types of marketplaces: major, intermediate, and minor. If two marketplaces meet on the same day, different family members may attend the different markets.

## MAJOR MARKETS

Three major markets serve the region. Redside, a primary major market is very large, including some 300 booths at the peak of the summer season. It is typical of major markets in the region with its great variety of goods, its volume of buyers, and its prime location.

The other two major markets in the region are similar to Redside in their composition and handling of goods. All three major markets are associated, respectively, with the three largest cities in the region. These locations provide sellers with easy access to wholesalers. It is in the major markets that most of the new goods appear from the cities. All three major markets are located on interstate highways.

### Redside Market

Redside Market is centrally situated in one of the most quickly expanding counties in the region. Its position on the highway makes it easily accessible to the country and the city. The majority of the sellers at the Redside Market live in the 10-county region. Virtually all license plates counted were from Redside's county or adjacent ones. The Redside Market is also used by a few long-distance sellers whose circuits include large markets in Florida, Georgia, and Michigan.

Originally the Redside Market was a tobacco warehouse. In fact, many of the older buyers and sellers still call it the Burley Barn, alluding to the days when it was a primary tobacco warehouse. When tobacco sales dropped, and federal subsidies were reduced, farmers began to offer used and reconditioned items for sale outside the tobacco barn, which was converted into the Redside Market in 1974. In its early phases, the market operated for only a few hours on weekends. In 1989 Redside

Market was open from 8:00 A.M. to 5:00 P.M. on Saturdays, Sundays, and Tuesdays.

The Redside Market site is on the major north-south interstate in the region, with a large billboard to announce its presence. The marketplace occupies some 10 to 12 acres, with plenty of room for expansion. Its parking lot alone can easily handle over 500 vehicles. Early in 1986 the parking fee increased from $.50 to $.75 per vehicle. The old tobacco barn, recently re-sided and with updated landscaping adding a modern touch to the exterior, covers about 25,000 square feet. The dusty high ceilings still retain the marks of tobacco stall numbers. Vendors begin arriving for the day's business early and slowly arrange their goods. Casual talk about the prospects for the weekend's business can be heard in the early hours. Since the cost of setting up a booth for the weekend is $40 ($25 for a single weekend day), sellers exhibit great concern about their profits. Fluorescent lights flicker in the dim barn, and cigarette smoke begins to fill the air. Vegetable vendors concentrate around the entrance and aggressively hawk their produce; as more and more buyers appear, the noise level increases to its eventual roar.

The number of booths varies with the season. In the winter well over 100 booths line the aisles of the marketplace in neat rows. Large, more-established booths with glass display cases fill the west end of the barn. These sellers constitute a permanent core in the marketplace. They attend the market year-round. On the few weekends when their booths are closed, cloths cover their tables and display cases, and a neighboring seller or family member will watch over the goods. Most of the vendors know one another; visiting between booths is the rule and the major mechanism for gathering information about business in Redside Market, as well as in the other intermediate and minor markets. Visiting is facilitated by the ease with which sellers can be relieved from their duties by kinspeople who share in the marketing work. In winter the eastern end of the barn contains small-scale sellers, who tend to be more itinerant. Their booths may consist of no more than a folding table with garden gloves for sale, or a couple of folding tables with ceramic knick-knacks produced in the basement of a farmhouse. By noon the indoor marketplace is in full swing with hundreds of patrons and sellers milling through the aisles, arguing over prices and visiting with friends and kin.

The goods sold at Redside Market can be described as including everything, even the kitchen sink. Used or reconditioned items from cleaned and polished pots, pans, and appliances to picture frames, china, and glassware are commonly found. A single booth might contain used clothing, handmade arrangements of dried flowers that have been collected and arranged in a vase purchased at another market, and a smattering of used dinnerware. The sources of the goods are as different as are their uses and pools of buyers. In a sense, one can see multiple livelihood strategies if one just considers the variety of the goods in a single booth. It is clear that many hours of labor have been put into reconditioning, repairing, and cleaning these goods. Booths may also contain such manufactured goods as socks, blue jeans, T-shirts, pencils, toys, watches. Many of the manufactured goods are cast-offs; that is, they are seconds or rejects or out-of-date items such as Christmas cards in January or Easter candy in May. Some of the booths are "branches" of small businesses: butchers, honey and vitamins, wood carving, antique furniture. Some of the businesses also occupy small stores in the urban Appalachian section of Cincinnati; others are located in basements in the shallow rural or in out-buildings on deep rural homesteads.

Within the period of fieldwork, we noticed striking changes in the numbers of sellers and in the kinds of goods sold in Redside Market. When we first began to study Redside Market in December 1985, it appeared to be a marketplace dominated by used goods such as trinkets, guns, farm equipment, and the like. Some new goods accompanied these things, but for the most part we saw a dominance of used and reconditioned items that represented added labor inputs on the part of the sellers. By July 1987 Redside had become more and more of a new and used goods market. The quantities of wholesale items, seconds, nonperishable foods, household items, and toys had increased, while the number of used goods had decreased. Whether this change represents a decrease in the supply of used things, or whether seconds and new manufactured goods became easier to obtain will be dealt with in a later section. Improvising in the marketplace becomes a necessary ability, and the variable composition of goods reflects both flexibility and change. One week a booth may contain a predominance of new things; another week it may feature new goods that were seconds, for instance, Levi jeans that were procured from a local distributor through kin ties. Several weeks later the same seller may clean out a relation's barn or come upon a cheap source of toys or watches. Thus, the nature of the goods in the marketplace can be quite variable.

Flexibility and a constant eye for the good bargain are probably the two most distinctive characteristics of the successful market vendor. Seasoned buyers know how to talk a seller down, an activity that seems to be enjoyed by seller and buyer alike. People who are tied into the system know how to bargain; strangers do not. More important, bargaining is one tool for obtaining items cheaply to resell.

Redside Market operates all year on a seasonal cycle. Summer is the busiest time, with stalls extending outside into the parking lot. The number of buyers increases, for summer tourists often stop. The amount of produce in the market increases in the summer, although wholesalers of produce operate on a 12-month basis. There were approximately five produce stands when the study began, a number that has remained steady with some increases during the summer months. The indoor regulars seem to resent the outdoor sellers because the rent is cheaper outside, and they compete for buyers.

A good example of a regular vendor is Mary, an elderly woman of some 70 years, who minds her booth that offers antique glass and china. Her husband, son, and daughter-in-law gather around her as the grandchildren dash into the booth to request money to buy french fries at the concession stand. Mary suffers from gout, and her son tells her that she should not have come to the market that day. She ignores him and speaks out to a buyer about the value of a piece of Depression glass. Family members repeatedly enter and exit Mary's booth as they ask her advice about a potential purchase from another booth. Someone asks, "Is that seller honest?" Mary replies with a bland answer and rearranges herself on her old rocker. Other sellers visit to inquire about her health. In the adjacent booth, a man named Jack sells costume jewelry. His prices range from $1 to $5 or $6. He works with the help of his teenage son, who actively recruits customers as they walk down the aisles. A bit further from Mary's booth, Will, a veteran of the marketplace system, stands in front of his own booth with five puppies for sale. There is no room for the puppies in the booth because it is packed with old appliances, bicycle parts, and crumpled copies of *National Geographic*. Will's adolescent children, a son and a daughter, tend the booth while he walks over to visit his father's stall three rows away. Will's father's booth has become a gathering place for men, mostly farmers. Talk about the prices of livestock and eggs can be overheard along with complaints about the new foreign-owned factories opening in the area. Will's father introduced him to the Redside Market.

The clientele at Redside Market is from the surrounding area. Many are market vendors who presently hold wage labor jobs; others are wage laborers or farmers who work in the area and who cannot afford to consume the expensive goods in the commercialized malls and chain supermarkets. There are many regular buyers at Redside Market, including large families. It is not uncommon to see parents purchasing shoes for five or six children or to encounter in the parking lot a station wagon with Ohio license plates containing nine or 10 extended family members. Often the families frequenting the marketplace from Ohio are migrants from Kentucky living now in Lower Price Hill, an urban Appalachian neighborhood in Cincinnati.

## Cardinal Crossing Market

The Cardinal Crossing Market, located in the northern section of the region, combines an interior shopping mall with an outdoor flea market. Since it is located near a large state park that draws tourists into the area, the market caters to visitors to some extent. The market may accommodate over 400 sellers on a busy day in the summer. For $10 per day, a seller can set up a booth in the outdoor section. New items may be present in the booths close to the building, but as one moves toward the periphery, the booths are filled with used goods. Often the booths with the used goods will also include seasonally available produce such as corn, green beans, and berries. These fruits and vegetables, reminders of rural economies, are indicative of the connections between subsistence goods and cash economies. The outside area, which is full during the warmer months of the year, can accommodate a large number of sellers, most of whom work out of the back of pick-up trucks. The outdoor booths are accessible to small-scale periodic sellers who use the marketplaces only sporadically, whenever cash is needed and when salable items become available to them.

## Greenville Market

The Greenville Market, located in the southern section of the region, is the largest and oldest major market. A billboard proclaims Greenville Market the largest flea market in the state. It operates on weekends year-round and is often very crowded. The market sits on a large gravel lot that has nine rows marked by signs posted on telephone poles. Electricity is available at each pole, but few sellers need electrical power. On very busy summer days, additional rows are created beyond the nine marked rows. These are lower-rent booths because they are so far from the entrance. The cheaper booths ($5 per day) are also used by small-scale vendors who deal in used goods, especially old car parts and farm tools.

Because the Greenville Market is outdoors, it is most active during the spring, summer, and fall months. Extreme heat and cold will stop all business. We visited Greenville on a summer day when the temperature reached 100 degrees, and only 25 of the usual 150 to 200 sellers were in operation. During the winter months, the Greenville Market moves from its outdoor location to a large barn about one mile from the outdoor site. A few hardy sellers, however, brave the cold and set up outdoors; these are mainly produce vendors. The winter barn has a capacity for about 50 sellers, but in late December only 15 booths were in operation. We were told by a seller that the market was ordinarily much busier but that after the Christmas holidays business was slow. In winter the market is open on both Saturday and Sunday, but Sunday is the busiest day. Small-scale sellers predominate in winter. Rent in the winter is $10 for Saturday and $15 for Sunday indoors and $5 for an outdoor booth.

The Greenville Market draws buyers and sellers from in and out of the region. License plates on cars and trucks reveal travelers from Kentucky, Tennessee, Florida, and many other southern states. Greenville is a favored stop on a larger market circuit that includes most of the eastern half of the United States. One husband and wife selling team in the Greenville market told us of their involvement in the larger circuit: they live in Florida during the winter months, where they sell produce. As the weather turns warmer, they pack a large truck with used goods and head north along the major interstate highway. The woman told us that her children, now all adults, often ask her where she will be. Her reply is, "You can find me somewhere along the interstates."

## INTERMEDIATE MARKETPLACES

Associated with smaller areas than are the major markets, intermediate markets are located along major county roads. There are at least five intermediate marketplaces in the region; only two will be described here. Intermediate markets are much smaller than major markets; they are much less commercialized and have fewer new items for sale. Intermediate markets tend to operate on a weekday rather than a weekend schedule.

Three teenage boys, all wearing baseball caps advertising farm machinery, stand in the bed of a pick-up truck. Spread across the tailgate and ground around the truck are used tools and household appliances, mainly files, hammers, hand-operated mixers, and plastic mixing bowls. A sign reading "green beans $1.00 a bucket" hangs from the truck. A man approaches the truck with a table lamp minus the shade and a bag of assorted goods. One of the boys asks him whether all three can go up to the auction. The man nods, puts the goods in the cab of the truck and begins to call out "beans a dollar a bucket." Across the gravel aisle, other trucks, campers, and station wagons also serve as market stalls. Several men form a circle and pass around some old shotguns one man brought to trade in the market. Guns are common items in the Webster Market, but they rarely appear in stalls. At the far end of the market, a woman sits on the hood of her car surrounded by ceramic salt and pepper shakers, gravy boats, and decorative plates. She tells us that she started setting up at 6:00 A.M. and that "some folks get here so early they have to set up with flashlights." Her things sell for between $.50 and $1, with a matched set of iced tea glasses and a pitcher going for $5.

She wants to leave the market but is waiting for her sister-in-law to return from the auction so they can pack up their goods. It is about 2:00 P.M., and most sellers are preparing to leave. Prices on produce are reduced; trinkets are put back in storage boxes; final sales are made; and children are rounded up by older siblings. The auction barn is also closing, and people collect their purchases, waiting for a friend or family member to pull a truck up to the barn for easy loading. People file down the concrete stairs from the auction barn to the parking lot market site. The man selling beans hawks his produce loudly as his three sons pack up the unsold goods.

## Breckenridge Market

The Breckenridge Market is an example of an intermediate market in the northwest portion of the region. It meets every Wednesday in the center of the town square. On market days the entire downtown area is filled with vendors. Temporary booths are the rule, and many of the town residents join in selling by setting up their wares in their front-yards. Many of the sellers we met at the other markets in the region were also present at the Breckenridge Market. This market is a favored spot with sellers and buyers alike because of the festival-like atmosphere of the town on market day. The market is advertised as an "antique" market, but it has equal amounts of new and used merchandise and draws from the same pool of sellers as the rest of the markets in the region. Summer is a busier time than winter, and this intermediate market usually houses between 25 and 50 sellers on a summer day. Intermediate markets lack the permanent characteristics of major markets; there are no permanent booths; rather the markets are usually collections of pick-up trucks lined up in gravel lots. They open at 6:00 A.M. and close by 2:00 or 3:00 P.M.

## Webster Market

The Webster Market is a popular intermediate market located 15 miles to the southeast of Redside Market, with which it is linked. Many sellers have both marketplaces on their selling schedules. The Webster Market is in the parking lot of a recently closed livestock auction barn. This auction barn was once the primary livestock trading site in the area and was part of a larger periodic system of livestock auctions.

The Webster Market consists of pick-up trucks and station wagons that fill available space in the parking lot. A new pattern of rows forms at every market meeting. The market begins at 6:00 A.M., and sellers use flashlights to set up and arrange their goods. Folding tables function as display areas, and merchandise may also be displayed on the ground or from the backs of vehicles. The set-up cost is $10. Most of the sellers are from the surrounding shallow rural area, and the ones with whom we spoke all lived within a 25-mile radius. The Webster Market operates throughout the year, although it is sparsely populated in the winter months, when sellers huddle around fires in trash barrels as they hawk fruit and produce obtained from wholesalers. The sellers who remain active at this time of year are also the men who trade in guns.

Because of the draw of the auction, large numbers of potential buyers come through the parking lot. Many of the vendors set up at the Webster Market not only to sell their goods but also to obtain access to the auction. While one family member tends the booth in the marketplace, others watch for goods at the auction. The auction is attended by experienced marketers who have long used marketing as part of a multiple livelihood strategy.

The auction facilities are used to buy goods for selling in the periodic marketing system. Goods are auctioned off by the truckload. The barn is a large structure that is unheated except for a few electric heaters hanging from the ceiling and a fire in a barrel in the center of the barn. The seats are arranged amphitheater-style and look down on a center ring, where items for sale are placed. The barn has two large garage doors on either side of the auction block so that sellers can back their pick-up trucks right into the ring. The auctioneer and a secretary, who records all sales and collects the money, sit on a bench about five feet from the floor.

On a typical day about 35 people sit in the barn, scattered around the seats and floor. People are engaged in conversation, but they always keep one ear on the business taking place in the auction ring. As the first truck backs in, a father and son in bib overalls begin to unload the items one by one. The goods include a sink; an eight-inch stove pipe; some electrical equipment such as wires, cords, plugs, and tape; some radiator cleaner; windows; tomato stakes; used farm tools; a water pump; an antique drill; and a 55-gallon drum. With the exception of the windows and the water pump (which the father decided to keep), most of the items brought on the truck were sold. The remaining unsold items were left in a pile on the floor for people to pick up free of charge. On this particular day, the father and son left the auction with $45 in cash. Other sellers generate much more money from their auction proceeds, from $65 to $85 per truckload. In a two-hour period, $300 worth of goods can be sold. Depending upon the specific goods, and the audience of buyers, even more cash can be generated.

The Webster auction functions as a distributor of a great range of inexpensive items, from old toys, clothing, farm tools, and old household items, to dishes and picture frames. It is not uncommon to witness a whole box of beautiful pewter picture frames, a dozen or more, being sold at the auction for a couple of dollars. One marketer will shine the pewter and then display and sell the frames individually, with or without photographs, for between $5 and $10 each. Old glass vases and wicker baskets, which people use to hold arrangements of wild and pressed flowers, sell for $.50 to $1. When finished, the arrangements sell in the major periodic markets and variety stores for $20 or more, sometimes as high as $35. The vendors collect the small items, such as the vases and baskets, combine the items with dried and pressed wild flowers, with perhaps a few cloth flowers obtained from a relative who works in a variety store. The value of the new product escalates geometrically, in large part as a result of the labor inputs and the creativity of the producers.

The change in the Webster Market through the period of fieldwork is noteworthy. From December 1985 to the summer of 1987, the Webster Market increased in popularity. By the summer of 1987, Webster was by far the most popular and well-attended intermediate market in the area. At the end of that same summer, the Webster lot was sold and the market and auction were forced to close because the new owner wanted to use the space as a parking lot for large tractor-trailer trucks. The amount of trucking in the area is significant, and the new owner thought he could glean more profit from parking than from marketing. After the close of the Webster Market, the Redside Market added Tuesday to its schedule and succeeded in picking up the Webster clientele. As a result, Redside continued the close associations that were so prominent in the Webster Market between the farm sector and the periodic marketing system.

## MINOR MARKETS

Scattered about the region in out-of-the-way places are numerous minor markets. Small and locally oriented, these markets are the most distant from the interstate highway system and are accessible only to the population of a small area. They are the most impermanent of all of the markets in the system. They meet primarily in the summer months and specialize in used and reconditioned goods. Many vendors offer homegrown vegetables in combination with other goods. The minor markets in Kentucky were usually set up in parking lots along secondary roads in the deep rural areas, although there is a minor market in a neighborhood in a highly urbanized area of a major city in the region. This area is close to the community of urban Appalachian migrants who came originally from the deep rural areas of Ohio and Kentucky. Along with urban goods such as televisions and typewriters, one sees produce and farm tools for sale. The market is set up in the parking lot of a large trucking firm in a heavily industrialized section of Cincinnati. The lot lies on a large and busy street. Several of the 20 to 25 sellers normally present at this market set up their wares in wooden stalls with roofs and wooden counters. Many of the sellers are retired or currently employed factory workers who have, or once had jobs in the industrial valley where General Electric and Proctor and Gamble have large plants. We spoke to a man in this market (Vale) who told us he was on vacation from his factory job and planned to spend as much time as possible selling in the marketplace. In the following case, the Willow Market provides an example of a minor market and its place in the regional periodic system.

## Willow Market

Honest John, a man in his sixties, has the most prominent booth at the Willow Market. A seasoned and successful marketer, he operates out of the back of a well-cared-for pick-up truck, offering new and used books, military paraphernalia, and baseball caps with small decorative clocks affixed to them. Honest John assembles these clock hats himself but sells them with the help of his "brother," who joins Honest John at many markets to entertain and draw shoppers into the booth. The market is in the side yard of a Willow community church, a grassy field with little shade. The sellers have arranged themselves in a kind of horseshoe. All of the church sellers cluster at one end and the "flea market people" at the other. The church started the market to raise money and also runs a concession stand, offering barbecue that several of the members of the congregation have made. Dave, a seller in his fifties, has a good spot in the shade where he sits with his home-grown tomatoes and new plastic housewares and looks hopeful when anyone nears his booth. The selling is slow, even for a minor market, and Honest John and his brother are catching what little clientele there is.

The Willow Market is the smallest of the markets we studied. It was established in the parking lot of a small rural church during the summer of 1987 and operated for only three months that summer. The market was initiated by the congregation of the church as a fund-raising project but was so successful that its operations were extended. The pastor's wife was aware of the popularity of marketing in the area and, therefore, thought that establishing a market by charging a "donation" of $5 to set up a booth would be a good way to raise money for the church. About half of the 10 to 15 sellers who tend booths in the Willow Market have been selling in other markets in the regional periodic marketplace system. In fact, the Willow Market became a regular stopping place for about six people who work in the regional periodic circuit. Their presence attests to the popularity of the Willow Market and to the rapidity with which it was linked to the regional system. Most of the flea market people sold used goods, but the two booths organized and operated by the church sold new goods, which were donated to the church by a large clothing manufacturer with outlets in Cincinnati. These new goods were priced much lower than similar items available in the regional system. After several weeks, many of the seasoned sellers had purchased the new goods, mostly pantyhose and winter clothes, from the church sellers and had them for sale at the other markets.

The Willow Market opened each Monday morning at 6:00 A.M., the only market in the regional periodic system operating on Mondays. The market was never crowded, but a steady flow of buyers came through until about 3:00 P.M. The market was located across the street from a public swimming pool, and many women with children crossed the street to visit the market. The slow, sultry afternoons at the Willow Market were often passed in conversation rather than in substantial selling activities.

Even though the Willow Market was planned as a short-term operation from the outset, it closed rather abruptly. When we went to the market one Monday in August, it was gone. Fluctuations in the sellers' and buyers' perceptions of "what is hot and what is not" (meaning where are the best places to sell) can radically alter the minor market to the point of closing it. Willow closed instead of changing its day of operation, an adaptation typical of other minor markets. The ephemeral character of these markets should not be mistaken for weakness or insignificance. The fact that minor markets can function in short time frames and that they can change locations provides flexibility for the multiple livelihood strategies.

# EIGHT

# *Using the Periodic Marketplace System* (with Sara Sturdevant)

This chapter centers on the differential use of the periodic marketplace system by families in the region. The use of the system varies not only according to the economic needs of people but also according to their position in the life course and their place in the family network. The three case histories below illustrate extensive, regular, and peripheral use of the periodic marketplace system, respectively. We have developed the typology as a sorting tool; that is, to organize what seems at first glance to be almost infinite variability among the sellers, the goods they sell, the particular marketplaces or sets of marketplaces used by them, the ages of the sellers, the kinds of help they receive from family members, the nature of their land resources, and so on. This typology is designed to aid in the understanding of multiple livelihood strategies by establishing the relative importance of market selling in the overall set of livelihood strategies used by families. The types represent distinctive categories of sellers and selling strategies. Someone interested in other kinds of research problems, for example, the characterization and analysis of behaviors in particular marketplaces, or the characterization of the kinds of goods sold, would need to develop a different set of categories, that is, a different typology altogether (Greenfield and Strickon 1986).

People who use the periodic marketplace system extensively devote large parts of every day to marketing or market-related activities. They pursue other livelihood strategies also, but the time they spend on nonmarketplace activities is relatively small when compared to their marketing activities. For example, in the case of Jane and Larry Rogers, illustrated below, they spend most of their time in marketing activities, but they are on the lookout for other sources of cash and have arrangements, in this case a house rental, that generate cash for buying subsistence items without a great time expenditure. In contrast to extensive marketers, regular marketers attend the periodic marketplaces each week, but they also devote significant amounts of time to other livelihood strategies. For example, in the case of Harry and Ilene Smith, significant amounts of time are spent in subsistence gardening and in performing odd jobs in addition to their marketing activities. People who use the marketplaces only peripherally have another primary or set of primary livelihood strategies; for example, tenant farming in the case of Mike and Amy Hooper.

## EXTENSIVE USE OF THE PERIODIC MARKETPLACE SYSTEM: JANE AND LARRY

For Jane and Larry Rogers, making ends meet has involved a long history of multiple livelihood strategies. Their schedule includes major and intermediate markets in a weekly sequence. They have been involved in the wage labor and service sectors and are linked to the rural economy in intricate patterns that involve efficient use of the subsistence sector by means of marketplace connections and the establishment of fictive kin ties that also generate cash.

Jane and Larry are both in their midforties. They live in a small town in the region, have been married for 19 years, and have a 10-year-old son, Danny. Danny has apprenticed himself to his mother by working in her booth in the Redside Market. He receives a dollar per day from her for his help. He is in charge of candy and cards, and his parents encourage him to use his profits wisely for reinvestment back into his "minibusiness." Danny's involvement is important for several reasons. His work is a real help to his parents as well as a means to earn cash for himself. He is involved in a family enterprise in a useful and meaningful way, and he learns not only from his parents but from other sellers. His presence is recognized and legitimate and provides him with both a strong sense of self and an opportunity to learn to handle money and responsibility. It does not appear that he is in training to become a capitalist but, rather, a small-scale entrepreneur.

Jane comes from a large family that includes nine full brothers and sisters and five step-siblings. She has 14 nieces and nephews. One brother lives on a producing farm in southern Kentucky, and she tries to visit him whenever possible. Two of her brothers and their families use the Redside Market. Jane's mother lives in Deep River, Kentucky, a community that is close to Webster. Her mother is raising one grandson, Jamie, now ten years old. Jane and other members of the family help her mother to care for Jamie by taking him to the dentist and running errands. Jane calls her mother daily. Jane's father lives in a southern Kentucky county.

In the late 1970s, Jane and Larry moved to a small (100-acre) farm outside Wallingford, Kentucky, which is located in the shallow rural part of the region. Having decided that it is too time-consuming for them to plant their own garden crops, they buy their produce from a seller at Redside Market. According to Jane, they can obtain their produce much more cheaply this way. Jane and Larry rent their previous house to a couple whom they describe as more like family than renters. We can see here a mix of commercial and reciprocal transactions within a system of neighbor, kin, and fictive kin relations (Bryant 1981). Jane spent the previous Thanksgiving with the renters, and they visit her frequently, often eating dinner with her. At the same time, Jane keeps careful records of their rent payments. She related that they had just paid her the fifty-sixth monthly payment, almost five years of rent. The rent is, of course, an important source of cash for Jane and Larry.

Jane and Larry became involved in the regional periodic marketplace system in 1984. Jane learned about the possibilities of selling in the marketplaces by helping some friends who worked a booth at the Greenville Market. Then Jane and Larry set up a booth on weekends at the Greenville Market. In February 1986 they opened their booth at the Redside Market, a booth still operated by Jane. In the summer of 1986, Jane quit her job as a cook and waitress, and soon afterward Larry stopped working for an insurance company so that they could devote more time to marketing. Jane and Larry now follow a weekly schedule that includes weekends at major markets, weekdays at various intermediate markets, and other time set aside for ordering merchandise, banking, and going to local garage sales and auctions to find salable merchandise. For the most part, the couple sells cosmetics and jewelry that are purchased through a wholesaler. Jane considers herself to be a good businesswoman. She always knows exactly how much money she has taken in at a given point in the day. We estimate her profits to be about $300 per weekend, and she compares herself favorably to other vendors in the market. In order to increase the size of her clientele and to increase her profits, Jane offers incentives to her regular customers such as raffles and bonus items for purchasing a given amount. Recently, Jane's booth at the Redside Market has expanded to include some new clothing and a collection of inexpensive costume jewelry. Larry travels to several markets in one week, as well as to regional fairs and other special events. His marketing activities require extensive traveling, so much so that Jane and Larry purchased a van that Larry could use for moving goods as well as for sleeping quarters. Jane stays at the Redside Market every week, and they depend on the steady income from her booth. She has developed a reliable and faithful clientele. Table 4 shows that Jane and Larry are together for two of their marketing days at intermediate

**TABLE 4**
**Extensive Use of Periodic Marketplace System**

|  | Jane | Larry |
|---|---|---|
| Monday | Run errands and acquire goods for the week | |
| Tuesday | Webster | Webster |
| Wednesday | Breckenridge | Breckenridge |
| Thursday | Order goods | |
| Friday | Attend garage sales to acquire goods for weekend | |
| Saturday | Redside | Cardinal Crossing or fairs on court days |
| Sunday | Redside | Cardinal Crossing or Greenville |

markets, but that they split up on weekends in order to cover two major markets.

Both Jane and Larry have decreased their involvement in the wage labor sector, although Larry always keeps his eyes open for part-time, temporary wage labor employment, especially in the winter months when market activity is slow.

For Jane and Larry, marketing or market-related activities absorb the bulk of their time. During many weeks their income is higher than it would be in the wage labor sector, and they have a great deal more time flexibility and freedom of mobility than had been possible for them in the wage labor sector. They speak freely about their decision to leave the wage labor sector. They made the decision to develop their marketplace activities in favor of what they view as "self-sufficiency," part of the Kentucky way.

## REGULAR USE OF THE PERIODIC MARKETPLACE SYSTEM: HARRY AND ILENE

We have met Harry and Ilene Smith already as residents of the shallow rural hamlet. They began selling as regular vendors in the periodic marketing system in 1979. Before that time they had been employed in the wage labor sector in various ways. Harry and Ilene have been married for 48 years. Both were born and raised in the same deep rural county in the region. They live in the shallow rural part of the region, but they have always kept in touch with their kin in the deep rural.

Throughout the week Harry and Ilene collect goods and process them for selling. They attend the Webster auction, minor markets, and garage sales. They take the goods, often after spending large amounts of time cleaning, repairing, and mending them, to one of the major markets on the weekend. As is the case for Jane and Larry, Harry and Ilene devote Fridays to acquiring goods from yard sales. They are very sensitive to market patterns in that they are careful not to spend too much time selling in one market. Ilene maintains that goods move faster if one uses several different markets in order to widen the pool of potential buyers. Ilene has a talented eye for bargains, and she can transform an old and dirty set of dishes into valuable antiques. One of Ilene's specialties (among many) is arranging dried flowers. She is the seller who combines the flowers she acquires from a relative who works in a Cincinnati crafts shop with ferns and flowers she has collected and dried herself. She buys the vases and containers at the Webster auction, in the minor markets, and at garage sales. On average, the total cash outlay for the arrangements is about $2. Her arrangements sell in the major markets for as much as $35. She is careful, however, not to deal in goods that require repeated time and attention. Clothing, for example, is something she assiduously avoids.

Recently, Harry has begun to specialize in guns and knives. These are popular items, but they require a much higher cash outlay to acquire than other used items sold by both Harry and Ilene. He previously sold used goods and trinkets, and the fact that he now concentrates on guns represents specialization for Harry and a selling plateau. He now makes more money than ever before in the marketplaces. He can risk the high initial expenditure on guns and knives because he is an experienced seller who has a network of people from whom he buys guns cheaply. He also has established a reputation for being an honest seller, and people come to him to buy and trade guns. The reputation for honesty is a sine qua non in gun trading.

On average, Harry and Ilene can count on $1,000 to $1,200 in cash generated from market sales per month. It is clear that their marketing incomes not only help to make ends meet but allow them a few luxuries as well. They use approximately half of the cash to pay bills and reinvest about half into purchasing guns for resale.

## PERIPHERAL USE OF THE PERIODIC MARKETING SYSTEM: AMY AND MIKE

Amy and Mike Hooper are a married couple who are tenant farmers in a deep rural county in the northern section of the region. They grow corn and tobacco and have a cow, several pigs, and some chickens. Both in their midtwenties, they have three children. The Hoopers were raised in the region and have kin living throughout Ohio and Kentucky. The couple is currently living in a small, one-story frame house with a large subsistence garden adjacent to the house. The house is located in the same area as Amy's mother, aunt, and grandmother, who share a small farmhouse, owned by Amy's grandmother, about a mile from Amy and Mike.

Amy and Mike were married as soon as she graduated from high school. Mike dropped out early because he "just didn't like it." They have moved several times in their seven-year marriage, but have always remained within the region. Amy's ties to her family, especially her mother and grandmother, are very strong.

Amy and Mike are included in the category of peripheral users of the periodic marketplace system because their participation in it is sporadic and makes a relatively small contribution to their livelihood. They set up a booth at Cardinal Crossing, a major market, once or twice a month and display about $25 worth of merchandise. Amy and Mike occasionally buy and sell at the intermediate Webster Market, approximately 50 miles from their home. Mike recently purchased a gun at the Webster Market for multiple purposes: to shoot squirrels and rabbits and to augment his treasured gun collection. Most of the goods they deal with are cut glass pieces and used kitchen utensils. The merchandise originates with Amy's family. Amy told us that her mother gives them the goods to sell and then asks for half of the profit. Mike complains that this is unfair because they have to pay the set-up fees. In the wintertime especially, these fees can be substantial at the major markets. Amy comments that marketing does not make them a lot of money, but the small profits they are able to turn over does help to make ends meet. Mike and Amy also buy toys and clothing for their three children while they are in the marketplaces. The two boys and one girl are permitted to play near the booth but must be escorted by their mother to visit other booths or to buy "treats." Mike likes the opportunity to meet other sellers, especially to talk about guns, a hobby of his.

Amy and Mike are unhappy about their position as tenant farmers but feel that there is little they can do to change their current situation. Mike has tried wage labor employment in the region, but he quit his job at the factory because he prefers to work outdoors. The Hoopers would like to own their own farm someday but doubt that they will ever have enough money to purchase land. Mike talks frequently about ways in which he might be able to make a lot of money quickly. He has considered buying the equipment for a Snow Cone stand but does not have the cash required.

Because of their low degree of reliance on the periodic marketing system as a source of cash, Amy and Mike choose to use markets that offer space at a low price. The summer outdoor aspects of major markets are suitable to their needs.

Peripheral sellers represent a large percentage of those involved in the marketing system in the region. This kind of small-scale selling comprises a cash-generating strategy that requires little capital investment and may be undertaken on a short-term basis. All of the markets in the system provide low-cost temporary booth space accessible to this type of seller. Goods collected from house cleaning (cleaning out basements and garages), craft goods, or goods gleaned from the kin network may provide the seller with sufficient goods to set up. Sellers from different households and families may also join together to sell, thus sharing the cost of set up. Often an individual will add his or her goods to those of an established seller and sell through that booth. In these cases price tags are marked with people's names or initials. In all of the above instances, the income generated from marketing is not substantial, but it may offer a welcome bonus to a household's budget.

The three couples above represent the rather high degree of variability among market sellers. They provide a picture of some of the different kinds of uses of the marketplace system in the context of multiple livelihood strategies. It is difficult to characterize the "typical" market seller. At the same time, these three examples alone indicate patterns in the use of the marketplace system. For example, Friday is a day devoted to acquiring goods to sell on the weekends in the major markets. The schedules people keep can be grueling at times, and missing lost opportunities can be costly in the long run.

## FAMILY NETWORKS AND MARKETPLACES

*Wilgus knew he couldn't live with his grandma in a daily way anymore. But perhaps he ought to stay nearby, live in walking distance of the house, secretly look in on her from time to time, keep a watch above her, do secret things to help her get along. Some mornings she'd get up and see her garden plowed, see her fruit trees pruned, her fences mended, and she would wonder: now just who on earth did that for me?*

*Norman (1977:17–18)*

The kin network is central to the way both buyers and sellers use the regional marketing system. Families provide the resources in both goods and labor for people to begin selling and to continue to sell. They also provide backup for slow periods by pursuing agrarian and wage labor activities that furnish cash and food.

## Mae

Mae is a regular seller who intensified her production of a craft product in response to a family crisis. Her livelihood strategies, if compared to those of other regular sellers—Harry and Ilene, for example—allow us to begin to draw conclusions about the nature of variability in multiple livelihood strategies among regular sellers.

Mae is a seller at Redside Market who comes from Potter County in the southern part of Kentucky. Potter County can be characterized as a deep rural area outside the region. She is 65 years old, married, and lives with her husband. She commutes from Potter County to Redside Market every weekend to sell quilts that she herself manufactures. The one time we noticed Mae missing from her booth in the Redside Market was the weekend a family reunion took place in Potter County.

Mae's trip to the Redside Market is a long one; it takes about three and a half hours for her to travel the 180 miles. It also takes her several hours to pack her truck on Friday night. She drives to Redside on Saturday, sells all day, and spends the night with her son who is married and lives in the shallow rural part of the region. Her son works in Fenwick Industrial Park. On Sunday, Mae spends another whole day selling in the Redside Market and then returns home Sunday evening.

Mae's involvement in the Redside Market has intensified recently. When Mae began selling her quilts, they were all handmade and priced between $150 and $200 each. She had a sizable clientele. Several years ago, her husband, who is retired from his factory job and who suffers from heart trouble, became very ill. Mae interrupted her commuting to the market to care for him. As the medical bills escalated, Mae and her husband decided to invest in a quilting machine, which would make the manufacturing process easier and quicker and enable Mae to produce more quilts. The quilting machine cost about $2,000.

Mae set up the machine in her kitchen and began to devote most of her time to the production of such quilted craft items as quilts, tea cozies, and potholders. Before she acquired the quilting machine, she produced fewer quilts. Her trips to the shallow rural area during this period had a dual purpose: to visit her kin and to sell what she could. When she began producing more goods, she spent more time selling in the Redside Market.

The prices for her quilts have dropped drastically because they are machine made. The quilts now sell for between $40 and $50. Mae's production has increased substantially, and she has now hired people to help her in the preparation of the material for quilting. Her booth at the Redside Market has grown. Consequently, she has rented more space in the marketplace.

## Scott

Scott, another regular seller at the Redside Market, has laid the ground-work for his two sons in the marketplace. Scott, a 62-year-old man, tends a booth filled with a mix of items. He sells used encyclopedias, small pieces of furniture, new pillows from a wholesaler, lamps, and so on. He has operated the booth for a long time, having opened it soon after the marketplace was established. He also owns a used furniture store, Scott's Bargain Barn, in an urban Appalachian neighborhood. When we first began talking to Scott, he appeared reserved, but his honesty and forthrightness came through as he told us his feelings about marketing. For Scott, flea marketing is getting to be too much work for the cash it brings. "People just want something for nothing," says Scott.

One of Scott's sons, Will, is a very successful seller. At the Redside Market, he operates a used item booth that is much like his father's. Will, who operates the booth throughout the year, is a popular figure in the marketplace. Men gather in front of his booth to chat and exchange information. It is bursting with such used items as old glasses' frames, bowls, jewelry, small appliances, old *National Geographic*s, and guns. We have seen Will at the Webster Market and auction, a good source of such items. With the help of his three children, Will also sells eggs from his farm in rural Ohio.

Will's son also works another booth on the same aisle several booths down from his father's. The booth contains new and used goods, including canned goods: soup, tomatoes, potatoes, and other staples. Will and his son move between the two booths, as do other family members.

Scott plans to give a substantial amount of merchandise to his second son, Jack, who is currently unemployed. When Jack takes over Scott's booth, Scott plans to devote more time to his furniture store. Members of Scott's extended family can always count on the fact that he and Will are present in the market.

## Ester and Walter

Ester and Walter, an elderly couple, represent a variation upon Scott's extended family pattern. They are the heads of a three-generation family network. While many of their kin are not marketers, they touch base with Ester and Walter each weekend to visit, to plan family dinners, and to organize the sharing of tasks.

Ester and Walter operate a booth containing used pots and pans in the Redside Market. The booth consists of several large tables that display an enormous variety of items, from the smallest saucepans to large electric frying pans, toaster ovens, and broilers. Their goods are known to be among the very best available, and they have placed labels on the goods

such as "just like new," "barely used," and "used only once" to attest to
their quality. They will take back any item that a customer considers to
be deficient in any way. This is only one aspect of their traditional de-
meanor. Ester, who wears black pumps and a cotton dress and apron to
the market, will explain the use of any of her very shiny and impeccably
clean items; she is proud of the work she has put into them to restore
them to "working order." Ester will trade items for cash, for other
goods, or for a combination of the two. She is a shrewd and serious businesswoman and knows when it is advantageous to talk and when silence is best. Walter, who dresses in bib overalls or work dungarees and
a baseball cap, keeps a watchful eye on the goods and will look after a
neighboring booth when the sellers want to take a break or visit another
booth.

   Ester and Walter are both in their seventies. In addition to their
booth, they operate a small farm near the Redside Market. They talk
about the rigors of maintaining their farmhouse: replacing windows,
keeping it painted, repairing the roof, and so on. The farm provides
them with produce for subsistence and is the homeplace for their children and grandchildren.

   As they sit in their booth on Saturdays and Sundays, Ester and Walter
are frequently visited by their adult children, who shop in the market.
One son, a truck driver, checks in with his mother to arrange the time
of Sunday dinner, a long-standing Kentucky tradition. They will eat at
his house after church services. Family gatherings solidify kin ties; they
ensure that people learn news of children and grandchildren who live
outside the region. These dinner gatherings also provide opportunities
for exchanging food, the "social glue" holding the kinship system
together.

## SEASONALITY

Added variability is introduced into the marketplace system by seasonality, which affects the goods that are available for vendors to sell,
the kinds of demands that are placed upon the goods, the kinds of markets in operation, and the buyers' and sellers' use of the marketplaces.
Summer allows certain goods into the market; produce for consumption
and for storage (canning). Outdoor markets, which are much less expensive for sellers to use, also flourish in the summer. A woman whom we
encountered selling at the Willow Market (a minor market) on the Monday after the Fourth of July weekend told us that she sold over $300 on
one day that weekend. She had been set up for three days at the Greenville Market (a major market) and was able to take advantage of the in-

creased number of tourists attracted to the market on the holiday weekend.

As the weather cools, the markets change. Outdoor booths will remain in operation as long as possible, but the number of booths begins to decrease in mid-October. Outdoor booths at the major markets contract. Minor markets almost disappear. Interestingly, the outdoor intermediate market, Webster, operates all year. Winter brings different kinds of goods into the market. For example, quilts, usually produced in the summer, sell well in winter. Produce sales focus on foodstuffs that will keep in root cellars and on basement shelves. Apples, onions, and potatoes predominate. Other subsistence items such as guns, hunting clothes, and traps appear, in addition to the increase of advertisements about hunting dogs. The Christmas season brings an influx of goods and people to the indoor marketplaces. Holidays, tax returns, and welfare payments all affect how sellers and buyers will schedule their use of specific markets. For example, people are most likely to buy at the beginning of the month when checks are issued.

In the winter months, the composition of families present in the market changes. While summer appears to bring family members into the markets as sellers, in winter, with the concentration of selling activities in fewer major markets, some family members will leave the markets to pursue other livelihood strategies. Many men take wage labor jobs in the winter or work indoors at renovating houses. People use their extended kin networks to produce items for sale in the winter months. Just before the Christmas and Easter holiday seasons, craft production becomes particularly important. Quilted items, ceramic figurines, ashtrays, such wooden craft items as birdhouses and potato bins, and jams, jellies, and honey and other home-processed foods abound in winter months. Winter brings a shift from intensive selling to intensive manufacturing. It also brings a flow of commercially produced goods into the markets; sellers who usually deal in used goods will add new items to their inventories. Because of the increased demand for toys, most booths offer some types of inexpensive games or dolls. Cosmetics and antique glassware are popular Christmas gift items. In sum, the Christmas season has a terrific impact on marketplaces in the region. Just as larger commercial commodity retailers are booming at this time of the year, so are the periodic markets.

## Mabel

Mabel, a 65-year-old woman who lives in a rural area in the northern part of the region, sells quilts in the Webster Market. She sells her machine-stitched and inexpensively priced quilts from the back of her van, an operation she runs with the help of her daughter-in-law.

Mabel manufactures most of her quilts in the summer. Her daughter-in-law aids her in piecing and sewing the quilts. The two women live near one another so they can work and still care for Mabel's grandchildren. They store materials in both of their homes. As fall sets in, the women prepare for the selling season which lasts through the winter. When spring arrives, they leave the marketplace and begin producing quilts for next winter's sales.

Mabel has arranged her marketing of quilts to take best advantage of the seasons. Heavy quilts do not sell well in the heat of the summer unless they are offered at extremely low prices. Mabel uses the summer months to manufacture a sizable number. In winter her time can be used to travel from market to market, and she can devote her time to selling without worrying about additional production. With the help of her family, she has the resources and additional labor to follow this seasonal pattern.

We have seen thus far considerable variation as well as continuity in the marketplace system as it fits into multiple livelihood strategies. The variability can be seen in the types of markets (major, intermediate, and minor) and in the types of sellers (extensive, regular, and peripheral). The continuities are strong, and they center around the maintenance of the family network as the primary unit of economic organization.

## Margaret

Margaret, a seller with a permanent booth in the Redside Market, plans her schedule to take advantage of the holidays. She has been involved in the Redside Market since its inception. The booth is filled with antiques she collected while operating an antique store in Covedale. In addition, her daughter operates a booth that also features antiques provided by Margaret.

Margaret is about 65 years old and lives on a small farm near the town of Easton with her husband. She has a daughter and a son, both of whom are now adults and live near their parents' homestead. The farm is located about one and a half miles from the secondary road, and Margaret proudly told us that the nearest neighbors live three miles away. Her large farmhouse has eight rooms, and Margaret stores most of her merchandise in the house. Several outbuildings hold what Margaret terms "a bunch of junk." Margaret saves everything.

Approximately four years ago, Margaret's husband suffered a heart attack. At that time Margaret found keeping the store open to be too much work: she could not put in the long hours required. The time flexibility offered by marketing provided Margaret with a means of generating cash on a more circumscribed basis. She could care for her husband during the week and then work selling at the market on the weekends.

We encountered Margaret in the market on a spring weekend. As we looked at her merchandise, she began to tell us about the decline in the number of sellers at Redside. She said that many of the vendors who sell at Redside in the winter were moving to outdoor markets such as Webster. According to Margaret, people moved to outdoor markets because the rent was cheaper, especially in the minor markets. Margaret described the Redside Market in the summer as "kinda slow." She told us that for a number of years she did not even sell in the summer because of the heat and the related fact that no one buys much at Redside in the summer. According to Margaret, wintertime is best at Redside. The market barn is well heated and is filled with sellers. By Christmas, business is really booming, and "you can't carry enough stuff out here to sell." Margaret expects the Christmas season to be her biggest selling time. She sells an increased amount of fancy glassware for gifts at that time. When asked whether the markets slowed down in the winter too much, she replied, "Oh, no. . . . that's a good time."

We should note that during the time Margaret was operating her antique store and helping her daughter run a booth at Redside, she was also working at the local hospital. She has been selling old things to generate cash for a number of years. It is clear that she has always operated with multiple livelihood strategies that are similar to others that we have described in this book. Marketing is an important aspect in that strategy. Her scheduling of time and labor inputs to marketing reflects changes that she perceives in the demand for her goods as well as obligations to her kin group.

In sum, it can be seen from the cases above that there is considerable variability in people's use of marketplaces. One way to understand some of the variability is in terms of the place of marketing in people's overall livelihood strategy. We have focused first on three couples who use the markets extensively, regularly, and peripherally. It should be noted here that both men and women in these couples participate equally, although not identically in market selling. Another variable affecting the use of the marketplaces is seasonality. This is a critical variable for a number of reasons, not the least of which is the seasonality of other work activities, for example, in agriculture and construction.

# NINE

# Generating Cash: Families, Factories, and Multiple Livelihood Strategies (with Sara Sturdevant)

*When Dean graduated from high school, he and Nancy already had a baby on the way. His father wanted him to go into the Army, to learn a trade, but Nancy didn't want to live at some strange military post with a new baby. She needed her mother at a time like that, she insisted. They had a difficult time starting out on Dean's wages at the filling station where he had worked throughout high school. Later, he worked at a garage and then for a while at the tire plant, where he made good money (nine dollars an hour). When Nancy started working, they were able to buy a two-bedroom brick ranch. The tire plant laid off half its force two years ago, and Dean started working as assistant manager at the downtown drugstore on the courthouse square. It was less money, but Nancy said she was glad, because the machinery at the tire plant was dangerous. "I was a nervous wreck," she told him. "But I wasn't going to get hurt," Dean insisted. "I knew what I was doing." The harsh rubber fumes at the tire plant burned his eyes, though, and the drugstore is more pleasant. Mr. Palmer, the owner of the drugstore, has treated Dean well, giving him a generous discount and free ice cream from the soda fountain for the kids. Medical advice from the pharmacist has saved them countless doctor bills. But before long, the drugstore will close, as soon as Mr. Palmer can sell it, and Dean will have to find a new job.*

*Mason (1989: 83–84)*

*"And what the land could not provide, hard cash would."*

*Norman (1977: 18)*

## METHODS OF GENERATING CASH

Various forms of wage labor—factory work, waitressing, temporary secretarial work, to name a few—interdigitate with the agrarian and marketplace economies in the region. Wage labor, whether it is permanent or temporary, is a means of generating cash that is used for purchasing goods people cannot obtain by any other means, that is, either through exchange with kin or by producing the goods themselves. Cash generated through wages is one, among many, sources of livelihood.

Many people who are employed as wage laborers are using, or have used, both "temporary" and "permanent" positions. The basic difference between the two "folk categories" of work is that permanent positions carry benefits, and the pay is substantially higher than the wages of temporary work for the same work tasks. The term "permanent wage labor" is somewhat deceiving in the sense that plant closings and layoffs are extremely common. People are well aware of the temporary nature of so-called permanent wage labor (Pappas 1989).

The attitudes and positions people hold about employment and preparations for loss of employment vary according to the extent of a person's family network and according to a person's position in the life course. Younger permanent employees have expressed fewer worries about loss of work at the industrial park than have older workers. Older members of the permanent work force have a strong belief that the wage labor available to them will soon disappear. These older workers are highly dependent on subsistence gardens, and many have been working to increase their involvement in alternative cash-generating strategies such as selling in marketplaces and performing odd jobs. As the previous chapters have shown, activities in the marketplaces enable people to gain access to goods through exchanges with other vendors. It is not uncommon for a wage laborer, who sells in the marketplaces on weekends, to acquire a 100-pound sack of potatoes from a fellow market seller for two or three dollars. The potatoes will be consumed by the person's nuclear family and perhaps also redistributed to other members of the family network who may be in need. Craft items that are produced by members of a person's family network commonly appear for sale in factories and in offices. Fellow wage workers are encouraged to "do their Christmas shopping early."

## Winslow Herman

Winslow Herman is a permanent employee at the Rinterline facility in Fenwick Industrial Park. Winslow, 45 years old, is married and has a daughter and two sons. He has been involved in the wage labor sector throughout his life and has been employed at the Rinterline Plant for about 10 years. Now a production-line supervisor, whose job situation seems to be rather stable, Winslow is always prepared for the closing of the plant. He is rather distrustful of the national economy, and he sees himself as a person who educates his fellow employees about how to cope with insecure jobs and low wages. Winslow stresses the importance of having a subsistence base to rely upon if the economy falters. His educational attempts have affected a few of the other workers, mostly younger men. Winslow has an organic garden that provides his family with most of its produce. The Rinterline Plant also employs temporary workers, who often work side by side with Winslow.

Many of the temporary workers have become disillusioned by constant job changes and the insecurity it creates. It is not uncommon for people to be hired for nine months at minimum wage, laid off for three months, and then rehired if the person's work record is good. Since, in the temporary wage labor system, no benefits are required to be paid, the people who work in management positions maintain that permanent workers are too expensive. Rinterline stopped hiring permanent workers in the early 1980s.

Workers with ties to agrarian economies are much better equipped to use the temporary labor system as part of a system of multiple livelihood strategies. Most temporary workers have told us that they regard this sort of work as a short-term strategy to fill time between jobs, to help out in "bad times," or as additional employment, meaning supplementary employment to either agrarian work or permanent employment.

## Moe Harley

The link between the marketplace economy and the economy of wage labor is primarily through consumption. Moe Harley is a 38-year-old temporary employee who obtained his job through the Coral Company, a temporary employment agency. Moe was born on his family's homestead in southern Kentucky in a deep rural area. As a teenager, he earned money hauling hay and produce to various marketplaces. His family lost their farm when the state appropriated the land for mineral rights. The family then moved to Covedale, Kentucky, in the shallow rural, to live with Moe's uncle who was in the priesthood there. They turned the uncle's entire backyard into a subsistence garden. Moe's two sisters were married and bought houses next to each other in Covedale. They began to care for neighborhood children in their homes and eventually opened their own day-care center. Moe's sisters purchase food and supplies for the day-care center regularly at Redside Market. Moe works at the day-care center occasionally. In addition to his temporary job in Fenwick Industrial Park, Moe sells metal items at the marketplaces. He uses the marketplace to purchase tools and fishing equipment as well as food and clothing. Wage laborers and their families commonly purchase goods of all kinds in the marketplaces. In fact, the kinds of goods featured in the marketplaces can be understood, at least in part, in terms of the needs of wage laborers. For example, the various companies in the industrial park do not furnish the temporary wage laborers with work uniforms. The abundance of used work uniforms for sale in the market-places can be understood because of the great demand for work uniforms below the ordinary commercial price. Clothing, especially children's clothing, and ordinary household items also can be bought at significantly cheaper rates, as can foodstuffs, although many people produce and process a large portion of their own food. For all these people, the extended family continues to be crucial in the overall system of multiple livelihood strategies. The roles played by family members, their work tasks, and their residential patterns vary from case to case, but the kin network remains the central organizing unit.

## Winnie Lewis

In the case of Winnie Lewis and her family network, wage labor is combined with continued ties to the agrarian sector that cut across the generations. Winnie's case is an example of the strength of kin: her biological family as well as her fictive kin relations with her employers, who have "adopted" her. Winnie herself has held many jobs in the wage sector. Her family, taken as a unit, is a model example of the ways in which all three sectors of the regional economy (agrarian, marketplace, and wage labor) are used to maintain the kin network.

Winnie Lewis is a 25-year-old woman who works as a waitress at a small, but very popular restaurant, The Old Wheel, on a state road approximately 15 miles from the Redside Market. She is an extremely personable woman who knows all of The Old Wheel's customers by name and who always seems to have time to stop and chat with people, even when the restaurant is extremely crowded. She works at the restaurant from 6:00 A.M. until 2:00 P.M., but she often stays later to help the owners clean up if they need her.

Winnie, the fifth of 11 children, was born in Cantor County in the eastern part of the region. Three of her siblings were killed in an automobile accident several years ago. Her parents moved to Cantor County from two counties in south-central Kentucky, part of the deep rural area. Her mother, one of five children, is 57 years old and a devout Baptist. Her 60-year-old father is one of 13 children and a member of the Pentecostal church. When she told us about her parents, Winnie stressed the importance of their religious affiliations. Both of Winnie's parents were raised on farmsteads that were sold when Winnie's grandparents died. Her father has a sister who remains in a deep rural area of south-eastern Kentucky and whom he visits at least once a year. Winnie's siblings are buried in her aunt's community.

Winnie's mother and father met in southeastern Kentucky and migrated north to Covedale, Kentucky, the largest city in the shallow rural area. They later moved to Neville, a small city east of Covedale on the Ohio River. After some time Winnie's parents were able to purchase a 69-acre farm in southern Cantor County. They have owned the farm, which includes an old farmhouse that is heated with wood, for about 30 years.

In Neville, Winnie's father found work in the steel industry. He has worked there throughout many phases of layoffs and rehirings. During the periods when he was not working in the steel industry, he worked more intensively on his farm, raising livestock (cows, horses, and pigs), tobacco, and a subsistence garden. When he was employed in industry, he continued to raise the garden. He is currently employed by the steel mills in Neville and also does temporary factory labor in order to keep his farm operating. He hopes to retire at the age of 62 and work his farm full-time.

Winnie's mother has always worked in the household and has processed food that is raised on their small family farm. The process of canning is tedious and labor intensive. After harvesting beans, for example, she must wash the beans, snap them, and blanch them. Jars must also be sterilized by boiling them. After the jars are boiled, they can be filled and closed securely, often with a rubber gasket, lid, and clamp. The filled jars must then be boiled again. Once the canning is completed, the jars must be arranged in storage areas. Winnie's mother also stores foods such as potatoes and onions. All of Winnie's five siblings help with chores around the house and the garden. They plant, weed, harvest, and help with canning the produce from the farm. All members of the family are proud of their capabilities in farming. Two of Winnie's sisters have moved away from the area and often joke about their city-dwelling mother-in-law who thought the brown eggs they gave her were dirty or spoiled.

Winnie's work history includes many jobs: from babysitting and dog-sitting to working as an answering service for a local funeral parlor. Her current waitressing job has social dimensions that are not easily seen. Winnie comments, for example, that she feels the employees at the restaurant are "like a second family; it is a home away from home." After her shift at the restaurant, she goes home, where she helps care for her younger siblings and pitches in with whatever household chores need to be done.

Winnie is divorced from a man who is in the military. Throughout her problems with the divorce, many members of the community gave her support. Neighbors allowed her to use their phones to call her husband, who was stationed overseas. Her employer at the restaurant offered to pay for a trip to visit her husband in Europe. After the divorce, she chose to remain with her family in Cantor County.

Winnie's parents cannot afford to pay regular prices for clothing and household items. Food is not a problem, since they produce most of their essentials themselves. The marketplaces provide the needed items at considerably cheaper prices than those found at the discount department stores and supermarkets. Winnie and her siblings have learned to combine the benefits of wage labor, farming (both commercial and subsistence), and use of the market as a way of generating and saving cash. Winnie commented that she is happy to see the Kentucky way of life documented. She is very proud of her parents' abilities to keep the farm in operation.

Winnie has now remarried. Leroy, her new husband, owns a small farm close to the restaurant where Winnie works. He was raised in Granite County, a deep rural county in the region, and his mother still has a farm there. He works in a hardware store in Allentown, located in Cantor County in the shallow rural, and does home repairs on the side (evenings and weekends). Leroy is divorced with one son who lives with his biological mother. There is much tension regarding increases in child support and jealousy on the part of his ex-wife. Because she was turned down for a loan on a mobile home, she is particularly bothered by the fact that Winnie and Leroy are purchasing a home. The ex-wife is not aware of the circumstances surrounding the purchase of the home, however. Winnie, as was previously noted, worked for some time as a dogsitter for a woman who was an employee of the railroad. When the railroad transferred her to Florida, she asked whether Winnie would be interested in purchasing her home, an A-frame with five acres in southern Cantor County. Because of their close friendship and their common residence in the county, the woman is selling the land and fully furnished house to Winnie and Leroy "for a song." Leroy moved into the house before Winnie and is cleaning and "fixin' up." Winnie jokes about his abilities as a homemaker and is very excited about planting her own garden.

Winnie considers herself to be fortunate on several counts. Both her restaurant "family" and her own extended family have provided her with support during her divorce. She also gives her respective families a great deal back in return. Extremely trustworthy and reliable, she puts in at least another workday in her mother's house after she leaves the restaurant. Clearly, the Kentucky way is part of Winnie's family's ideology. They also practice the Kentucky way every day as part of their regular series of activities. Their commitments to one another, their abilities to perform a myriad of work tasks, their willingness to help one another under all circumstances are only some examples. They also have strong ties to the land, ties that give them a sense of control over their lives and a place with which to identify.

Winnie's involvement in the factory wage labor economy has not been as intense as that of other people, however. The following two cases illustrate involvement in temporary factory work after a period of permanent work. For the two men described below, temporary wage labor provided them with a way to make ends meet by generating needed cash when permanent work was unavailable. For neither of the two men, however, were their wage labor jobs their sole, or even their primary, source of livelihood.

## Chester Smith

Chester Smith is 52 years old and lives with his wife, daughter, and two sons in Ulster, Kentucky, a small town not far from Fenwick Industrial Park. They keep a garden, and Chester goes hunting and fishing whenever he has the chance. The eldest son is employed at the airport by a major airline, while Chester is a temporary employee at the Rinterline Plant in the industrial park. Originally from Potter County, Kentucky, near the Tennessee border, Chester and his family lived on a farm. After his mother refused to allow him to enlist in the military, he sold his cow in order to purchase a used car to go to Cincinnati to live. Some of Chester's family are still in Potter County, where his two brothers still operate the farm owned by his mother. Chester visits the family there at least once a month.

In Cincinnati, Chester found a permanent job at which he worked for 25 years. He was then laid off and was forced to seek employment through a temporary service. At this time his wife also looked for and found a wage labor job which she still has. Chester was hired as a temporary employee at the Rinterline Plant, but was laid off in June 1987. At that time he went to Potter County for an extended visit. While there, he made some improvements on his mother's house.

Chester uses the minor marketplaces frequently as a buyer and a seller. He sells small pieces of furniture, household items, and "old stuff." Chester has commented that the more commercialized Redside Market is "just too expensive."

Chester's pattern of visiting his mother's farm once each month is not an atypical pattern in the region. It is not at all uncommon for people to travel some distance to visit relatives in the deep rural parts of the region as often as once per week. Harry and Ilene Smith alternated weekly visits to their respective parents when they were newlyweds. Chester's pattern is similar to the visiting patterns of one of the urban families whom we will meet in chapter 10. For the urban family, however, the pattern of traveling to visit relatives on farms in the deep rural is problematic because the distance is great and their stay is so extended. They develop a pattern of bilocal residence. In their particular case, trying to maintain two residences means that they try to live in two places simultaneously. Truancy for schoolchildren and job absenteeism for adults are some of the consequences. For Chester, however, the monthly visiting pattern is not problematic because it does not disrupt his regular pattern of multiple livelihood strategies that are already in place. While he uses and relies upon resources and help from kin in the deep rural, he can make ends meet without staying for a long period of time in the deep rural. That is, Chester can maintain his ties with family in the deep rural and obtain social support and economic resources from them without jeopardizing his overall pattern of livelihood. He is not cash dependent. In other words, all of his essential resource bases are already in place in the shallow rural. His visits are not a critical part of his livelihood strategy. However, the visits are critical to his mother: he fixes her house, meets kinship obligations, and maintains his homeplace ties.

## Spence Taylor

Spence Taylor is also a temporary employee at the Rinterline Plant in Fenwick. He is 44 years old and married with two teenage boys. The family lives in Tyson Meadow, Kentucky, another small town near Fenwick. Spence moved from southern Kentucky about 24 years ago after the deaths of his parents, who owned a producing farm in this deep rural area. When his parents died, Spence and his only sibling, a brother, divided the farm and sold it. Spence used his earnings from the sale of the farm to move toward Cincinnati (but not to Cincinnati) to seek employment. His first job was with the J. C. Container Company in Covedale, Kentucky, in the shallow rural area. He was employed there for 20 years and was then laid off. His wife then found permanent employment as a housekeeper at a local hospital, a job she still holds. Spence then looked for temporary employment at the Rinterline Plant. He was hired and then laid off from Rinterline in early June 1987.

Spence says he chose to live in Tyson Meadow because of the wooded area nearby where he planned to hunt and fish. Unfortunately, the area was developed into a housing subdivision. The Taylors keep an elaborate vegetable garden. Sweet potato clippings from the garden serve as decorative house plants. Spence's wife processes their produce and then stores it either by canning or freezing. The family also raises hunting dogs to sell.

Spence and his family use the flea market as consumers. He buys the household's weekly groceries at the Redside Market. Items such as soap and cleaning supplies, brooms, as well as cooking oil and salad dressings can be obtained for a fraction of what these items would cost in local supermarkets. Spence also likes to comb the markets for used goods and collectibles. An old plow that he found in an antique booth sits in the frontyard of the family's Tyson Meadow house.

We can see from the case histories of Chester Smith and Spence Taylor that they began their adult lives with ties to the deep rural and that they migrated to the shallow rural where they both held permanent wage labor jobs for 20 years or more. As they became older, their use of temporary wage labor, hunting and gathering, and consuming goods in the marketplaces increased. Temporary work was not stressful to them because they combined it with other work and because they were not seeking advancement. The tolerance of these two men for temporary wage labor is certainly not universal in the region, however. The young man, in the case illustrated below, spoke vehemently about the drawbacks of the wage labor system and quit his temporary wage labor to work odd jobs instead (cf. Rubin 1976).

### Nathan and Sue

Nathan, now 28 years old, was born on a farm in southern Indiana. From the age of 14, he worked as a carpenter's apprentice for a man with whom he had an excellent working relationship. The carpentry business was good, and Nathan worked extremely hard. At the age of 21, Nathan moved to Cincinnati, where he worked as a permanent wage laborer for a wholesale food company. When the food company went out of business, he went to work as a temporary wage laborer for the Goody Company, a large manufacturing firm, where he held a similar kind of job maintaining machinery and operating a fork-lift truck. He obtained this temporary job from an agency in suburban Ohio. While working for the Goody Company, he met his present wife, Sue, who is also 28 years old. She held a temporary job as a quality lab supervisor that she acquired through another temporary agency located in Fenwick, Kentucky. Her assignment ended in November 1986: the project to which she had been assigned was successful, and the product had been thoroughly tested. The next stage of the project was sent to Saudi Arabia and Japan. All temporary employees were notified of termination. Nathan and Sue were married in December 1986, and both of them renewed their search for employment. Sue quickly found another temporary job at the Rinterline Plant; she was anxious to find work because, as newlyweds, "there was the issue of cash flow."

Sue's first assignment at the Rinterline Plant was in a warehouse for automotive parts connected with a facility that disassembles and recycles used truck parts. She was placed on the United Parcel Service line. Fork trucks would bring huge pieces of automobile and semi (truck) parts up to the UPS packing area. "I hated it," she told me. "I had to figure out how to parcel things weighing 70 pounds—I weigh 104!" Most of the women (permanent workers) who worked in the UPS area were older and came from Granite County, a county in the deep rural part of the region that is a 45-minute drive south. "They were so incredibly *cheery*," she said. "I thought Rinterline was grueling—a curse; they believed in Rinterline." The UPS area of the plant was a "status symbol" and considered "cakey" by other employees who worked out in the body of the immense Rinterline Plant.

On several occasions, Sue was asked to drive fork trucks. She told me that her first reaction to this prospect was, "Oh my Lord!" The trucks were hard for Sue to master. "I recall nearly tipping one (over) trying to get used to backing up with a heavy load. I had never driven one before. I have my fingers crossed that no one asks again!"

Approximately one month into Sue's employment at Rinterline, she learned of a few openings in the machine recycling area. She told Nathan about these jobs. He applied and was immediately hired because of his machine operator's experience at the Goody facility. Because Sue and Nathan were temporary employees, they could both be hired at Rinterline. Permanent employees could not suggest to their spouses that they apply for either a permanent or a temporary spot.

Nathan's job in truck-part recycling at Rinterline was dangerous and dirty. Everything in this area of the plant was covered in grease. As a temporary employee, Nathan had to furnish and wash his own work clothes. In this particular work area, a set of clothes lasted approximately two weeks. The wage was $4 per hour. Sue told me that Nathan was exposed to petroleum products and that no mask was provided. She also said that the chemical compounds used to clean the recycled parts nearly ruined Nathan's wedding band. The floors were slippery from the grease which made it difficult to move 70-pound parts from one station to another. Nathan's back became very sore from several bad falls on the floor. Since grinding metal was part of the job, goggles were provided by the facility. The metal particles were so small, however, that they still occasionally came behind the goggles. Three weeks into his employment, a piece of metal slipped into Nathan's eye. He was taken to an eye doctor in Fenwick who removed the fragment. The doctor told Nathan and Sue that the eye was severely scratched, placed a patch over the eye, and sent Nathan back to work. Rinterline paid for the physician's bill, but did not "give Nathan a break work station wise," Sue told me. She said over and over again, "Nathan really hated Rinterline. He would look out the back door and exclaim that Fenwick had been converted into moonscape—all trees plowed down and only brown grass remaining, horizon dotted with factories instead of farms." Nathan himself said to me that he "felt dirty, like a peon! I know I can do better for myself."

Nathan walked off the job after four months as a temporary wage laborer. He called the temporary agency and told them he was leaving. He began self-employment as a painter and carpenter. Much of his work, especially initially, was obtained through connections long established by his father-in-law, Harry Smith (see chaps. 5, 8).

People, particularly men, who quit their wage labor jobs in favor of odd jobs or who decide to intensify their activities in the agrarian and marketplace sectors, often see themselves as "opting out of the system." Statements, particularly in the context of temporary factory work, such as, "I refuse to do the same job as the guy next to me and get paid half as much," became familiar refrains. Discussions about the dangers of factory work, the lack of concern for safety on the part of owners and managers came out in almost every case. People saw themselves as resistant to factory work, but their resistance took many forms. Sometimes criticism of fellow factory workers for not learning how to plant gardens, for wasting time and money on beer and partying instead of spending time with family became the idiom of resistance to temporary wage labor. It was clear that people saw their "investments" in kin networks as providing them with flexibility, with options to leave wage labor jobs and establish other means of gaining their livelihoods. In many instances the bottom line was simply to survive in the face of constant layoffs. In the cases that follow, people take on temporary wage labor at the beginning of their adulthood rather than at the end. Problems or potential problems can be predicted.

## Lila Thomas

Lila, a 26-year-old college graduate who lives and works in the shallow rural part of the region, was born in Kay County, Kentucky, as were her parents. Her maternal grandparents were farmers in Georgia, and her paternal grandparents were farmers in northern Kentucky. Her father operates an independent plumbing company in the region, while her mother has used the temporary employment services since 1985.

In 1987 Lila took a temporary job in Fenwick Industrial Park. After five months, she was hired as a permanent worker, a situation that most temporary workers desire but one that rarely occurs. Lila's eldest brother is a plumbing supplies salesman. Her next eldest brother has graduated from college and has been using temporary employment services for the past three years to find work. Registered with five agencies in the area, he was still unemployed at that time.

Lila states that the family is on a tight weekly budget: "I believe we are currently statistically below the poverty line, but we do okay." Her mother's weekly wage from her job at Fenwick Industrial Park keeps the family solvent. The family has a garden, and Lila's mother bags and sells in the regional marketing system on a regular basis. She describes her work in it as a hobby, but it is clear that her activities in the market-place allow the Thomas family to save as well as to generate cash. Mrs. Thomas buys clothing, food, and household goods and sells crafts that she produces at home.

Lila is now registered with four temporary employment agencies in the region. She has had 15 different assignments since June 1985. Lila laments that her experience with the temporary wage labor market has been less than satisfactory and adds that temporary workers receive no benefits. She is particularly unhappy with the insecurity of her job and with the fact that temporary wage labor offers virtually no chance for advancement. "You never know exactly what you will be walking into as the companies and the temp services often cross wires." She said that she has often been told that she will be performing one type of duty and then is assigned to something completely different when she arrives at the workplace. The type of work assigned to Lila thus far on her temporary assignments has not been helpful in allowing her to build her skills so that she might be able to find permanent work. She states that "nine times out of ten what you learn on a new job will have no bearing on anything else you will ever do in your life." The attitudes expressed by permanent employees toward temporaries are often derogatory and unpleasant. Lila says that "sometimes it feels as though you are a second class citizen," and she hopes to get out of the temporary wage labor market as soon as she can. "I want to go back to [graduate] school, and I want to grow a vegetable garden for my subsistence. I see temporary services as a last alternative, but I have, obviously, been grateful for their existence."

## Rachel Stewart

Rachel Stewart is 24 years old and lives in a small town in the deep rural part of the region about a 45-minute drive south of Fenwick. She has been married for three years to Clyde, who is employed as a truck driver. Rachel holds two wage labor jobs simultaneously. She works full-time in a quality control lab of one of the largest companies in the region. She works this job on the first shift. At night she works part-time in a jewelry store in Fenwick Mall. Rachel talks openly about the stresses of her situation. She awakens at 4:30 A.M., fixes breakfast, and must be at work by 7:00 A.M. She has a 40-mile commute to work, a drive that can be extremely hazardous in wintertime. She often passes her husband on the road, and they beep "hello" to each other.

Clyde and Rachel live in a mobile home on her father's farm, which has a tobacco base. In the fall Rachel spends considerable time processing tobacco. Her father once worked the farm on a more or less full-time basis, but now he sells TV satellite dishes and is a Fundamentalist preacher. The reasons why her father diversified his livelihood strategy are not all clear, but the decrease in the tobacco subsidy has caused tobacco to yield much less cash than formerly. It is not uncommon for people who once worked either as full-time wage laborers or as farmers to develop several different livelihood strategies in later years.

Rachel says that she does not want any children because the economy is "too tough." As we can see, her work schedule is a grueling one, and even though she has an extended network of kin to help her with children, her cash earnings appear to be essential to her and her husband, as well as to other family members. She enjoys living in what she calls "the country" and says that she would never move to the city because she does not like the fast pace. This statement should be interpreted in light of the hectic schedule that Rachel normally keeps. She has close ties with her in-laws. They live close by, and Rachel describes them as being "close knit."

## Jenny Smith

Jenny is a 35-year-old temporary employee at a large factory in Fenwick Industrial Park. She has been married twice. Jenny is familiar with urban institutions of higher education, since she has taken numerous college courses and her first husband was working on his Ph.D. in chemistry at the university. They were divorced in 1978 when their son was seven years old. Her second husband, Tim, is a farmer from Grange County who is employed at a large automotive plant in Notwater, Ohio. He has two children from a previous marriage.

Tim did not want Jenny to work in the city because he feared the contact that she might have with other men. Before taking her present job, Jenny worked in a Cincinnati office using computers, a skill she learned in the college courses she had taken. Tim attended an office party, discovered that her male boss was "good looking," and forced Jenny to quit her office job. Her job in the industrial park was acceptable to Tim because all of her co-workers were female and her work schedule allowed her to fix his breakfast for him. Jenny says that Tim is very traditional.

Tim has worked at the automotive plant for 18 years. (The plant closed in August 1988.) He earns $26,000 annually. He continues to farm, however. Jenny says that "farming is in his blood." In 1985 they raised 220 pounds of tobacco. They worked at processing the tobacco well into January. They have considered farming full-time if he ever loses his job. Farming was attractive to Tim and Jenny because it would bring them a certain degree of self-sufficiency and control. They would no longer be in the chain of command as in the factory or the office workplace. Jenny does sell homemade Christmas crafts to the people in her office as another source of cash, but she viewed her combined income from her office and craft work as supplemental to the household income. This is another way of saying that she felt herself to be in a subordinate position.

Jenny has more education than does her second husband. She had taken courses in computer technology at a community college and has used these skills in her office job. Tim was resistant to her educational pursuits. She told us he tried to please her with material possessions, such as a microwave oven, to "keep her happy."

Jenny's ties to family members were very important to her. She is close with her sister, and they communicated with one another frequently. She "lost" the relationship with her parents and was very unhappy about this. Her father is an alcoholic. They still have a farm, but Jenny rarely visited.

In 1985, Tim left her. At the time he acknowledged that she had been a good wife but that he just wanted a younger woman. She lost the house they had lived in and the insurance benefits that her husband's job had provided. Jenny and her son then moved to an apartment. Soon afterward the firm for which Jenny worked began to lay off workers. Jenny was especially fearful for her job because she was one of the last hired and was a temporary worker. She was laid off in July 1986 and was unable to find other work.

Jenny became severely depressed, although she put up a happy front. She was admitted to the psychiatric unit of a local hospital in August 1986. She told all of her visitors not to worry and that everything was going to be fine. She was released after a three-week stay. Several weeks later, she was found dead in her apartment of a drug overdose.

## SUMMARY

For Jenny the absence of alternative livelihood strategies makes it impossible for Jenny to manage. In part, that lack of varied livelihood strategies is a function of the fact that she is cut off from her parents and their family land. Without the support of a full family network, it became impossible for Jenny to continue. The last three cases in this chapter deal with increasing reliance on cash and the wage labor economy. For some people factory work is tolerable because they do not see themselves as factory workers or as completely dependent upon wages. Factory work is only one component of livelihood for members of kin networks. In most cases families maintain access to agrarian resources. In several cases the kin network provides other options for jobs. For Lila dependence on temporary wage labor is unsatisfactory because it does not meet her image of her own self-worth. For Rachel increased reliance on cash requires a grueling work schedule, but support from her kin network makes the schedule bearable.

# TEN

# The Breakdown of Multiple Livelihood Strategies

*"He wanted a job and there was none. He said he was leaving to go live in Cincinnati. Everyone was upset. They said he should stay. I recall my grandmother crying. I asked my mother why. . . ."*

*She and her husband Tim and their five children had gone back and forth for years, from Harlan County to Dayton, Ohio. They tried living in Chicago too. "We had a terrible time in Chicago, and I think it hurt my children for life. We were away from all our kin. We were afraid of the streets there. And I had to work along with my husband. We came there to make as much money as we could. We hoped that we could save some, and then go back to Kentucky and maybe work some land that belongs to Tim's daddy."*

*Coles and Coles (1978:79)*

*"While the water glugged out over the sweet peas I noticed Mattie looking at me with her arms crossed. Just watching. I missed Mama so much my chest hurt."*

*Kingsolver (1988:81)*

*"She was quiet for a minute. The hiss of the steam iron and the smell of warm, damp cotton reminded me of Sunday afternoons with Mama."*

*Kingsolver (1988:101)*

Two families migrated from the deep rural parts of Kentucky and Tennessee to an Appalachian urban community in Cincinnati, a migration that is atypical of most such moves throughout the world. The families in these two cases have migrated to a city in which they have no kin. In this chapter I analyze the breakdown of multiple livelihood strategies as a function of the inaccessibility of kin. The costs of this migration pattern are so great that kin networks are stretched to the breaking point.

Two case histories of hospitalized Appalachian adolescents in an urban university teaching hospital provide some insight into this breakdown. Since the vantage point is that of an inpatient psychiatric unit, the specifics of the cases represent extremes to a great degree. At the same time, the family histories are not at all atypical for Appalachian families. The difficulty of maintaining the supports and obligations to traditional extended families under urban conditions is mirrored in the problems of the adolescents. The focus here is not on mental health issues, however—although these are certainly not to be dismissed as they are revealed in the case histories—but on problems of livelihood.[1] The psychiatric cases should be understood as special lenses that magnify dynamic relationships between multiple livelihood strategies, family structure and homeplace ties, and rural-to-urban migration patterns.

It must be clear at the outset that I am not arguing that the breakdown of economic strategies causes psychiatric disorders. The dynamics of the case histories are much too complex for such an argument. In keeping with our comparative perspective, it should be mentioned that the cases illuminate economic and family relationships and processes of change that are by no means unique to the Appalachian region.

The case materials for this chapter were collected as part of a research project that involved the adolescent psychiatry inpatient service of an urban university teaching hospital in our Appalachian region. The city of Cincinnati has received Appalachian migrants from rural counties in eastern Kentucky, West Virginia, and Tennessee, as well as from rural Ohio. Most of the patients on the unit are poor and have, in psychiatric terms, family systems that are dysfunctional in their present environments. Of the approximately 136 adolescents between the ages of 13 and 17 hospitalized on the unit each year, about 20 percent come from families that originate in rural Ohio, Kentucky, Tennessee, or West Virginia. On average, the adolescents stay in the hospital for one month.

## TWO CASES OF HOSPITALIZED ADOLESCENTS

I focus upon two detailed case analyses of hospitalized Appalachian adolescents. Both patients are young women from rural Appalachian backgrounds. Both adolescents are first-generation urban residents from poor families, who were part of the most recent stream of rural-to-urban migration (McCoy and Brown 1981; Philliber and McCoy 1981; Schwarzweller and Brown 1970). The two patients have typical problems (Danna 1980; Brody 1970). The patients are not delinquents, chronic substance abusers, criminals, or violent individuals. Neither patient is psychotic and neither has a major mental disorder, such as schizophrenia or bipolar affective disorder. I chose two young women to highlight patterns of behavior between parents and children and to draw similarities as well as contrasts between rural agrarian and rural wage labor backgrounds. I pay particular attention to the adaptation problems (economic, cultural, and psychological) of the mothers of these adolescents, since their problems contribute to their daughters' inabilities to function. The patients and their mothers make repeated visits to their rural places of origin and, in fact, try to live in two places simultaneously. Thus, the importance of homeplace ties becomes a major issue in these cases. What these homeplace ties represent in economic terms, and how the economic and family issues intertwine in the breakdown of multiple livelihood strategies, will be treated below. For purposes of confidentiality, the names and some of the symptoms of the patients have been omitted or changed slightly.

## Teresa White

At the age of 16 Teresa White was hospitalized for six weeks. One month before she was admitted to the hospital, she took a drug overdose. Six months prior to admission, she dropped out of school. Teresa is one of six children. Her 19-year-old sister is unmarried with a two-year-old child and is reported to have a drug problem. Teresa's 17-year-old brother has drinking problems, and her two younger brothers, ages 14 and 10 have been reported by the community social worker to have school phobia. Teresa and her brothers live with their mother, who has been divorced for seven years. Her father is an alcoholic who lives in Florida.

Teresa's mother grew up on her family's farm in Tennessee. She migrated to Cincinnati because she felt the move would increase her economic opportunities. Teresa's mother pursued jobs with some energy, but she seemed unable to keep a job for longer than a few months. When Teresa was admitted to the hospital, her mother was working for the Salvation Army.

Mrs. White's health problems contributed to the mental health problems of her daughter. She complained of back pain and would frequently take off from work or quit her job to retire to bed. The back pain seemed to be chronic; medically, no known organic cause could be found. She always had the intention of maintaining a job "as soon as her back was better." During her times in bed, Mrs. White would ask Teresa to stay home from school. When she was not working, Mrs. White received monthly checks from Aid to Families with Dependent Children (AFDC). She moved frequently from one apartment to another within the urban Appalachian area. She never lived in an apartment with a phone.

Teresa's paternal grandmother, maternal grandmother, and maternal step-grandfather lived in Tennessee. Throughout the year Mrs. White and the children traveled to the Tennessee farm. Whenever they felt that they could not cope with their lives in Cincinnati, they left for the farm. Their visits occurred as often as once a month or more. The farm consisted of several dwellings on a homestead, a garden, and some livestock.

Mrs. White took every available opportunity to go to the farm. She said that she felt she needed to take care of her mother. When one of the grandparents had a heart attack, Teresa's mother packed up her children to move back for a long stay. The precise amount of time the family would spend away from Cincinnati was always left ambiguous. Mrs. White often told everyone that they were staying for the weekend, but in actuality they would stay at the Tennessee farm for a few weeks. On average, Mrs. White and the children would travel to the farm a dozen times each year. The family talked about the grandparental homeplace (the farm) as the "real" home for them. In effect then, Teresa's nuclear family was biresidential; they maintained two equally important residences throughout the entire year.

One of Teresa's main difficulties during her hospitalization concerned her anxieties about leaving her mother. Teresa was afraid that something awful would happen to her family during her absence. Teresa's therapy included individual, family, and group sessions to diminish her fears and depression and to strengthen her mother's ability to function as a parent.

## Mary Lou

Mary Lou is also 16. She was referred by her school to a psychiatric clinic because of a school phobia. At the first session, she told the psychiatrist that, if forced to return to school, she would kill herself. Because of the suicide threat, she was hospitalized on the university hospital's inpatient adolescent psychiatric service.

At the time of her admission to the hospital, Mary Lou lived with her mother, stepfather, and toddler stepbrother in an urban Appalachian neighborhood. She was born in a West Virginia coal-mining town, where her biological father had worked in the mines. Her grandmother took care of Mary Lou while her mother worked. Her mother was divorced when Mary Lou was six months old; she remarried shortly thereafter. After the divorce, Mary Lou's biological father went to live in Kentucky, while Mary Lou, her mother, and stepfather migrated from West Virginia to Cincinnati. The move was precipitated by her unemployed stepfather's need to work.

Mary Lou was the first person in her family to enter high school; her mother had completed the eighth grade. Mary Lou started her grammar school education in West Virginia, where her grandmother expected perfection. If she brought home an A, her grandmother would demand to know the exact number grade and would question her if her score was not 100. Her grandmother treated Mary Lou as someone special, and Mary Lou felt disappointed when she could not meet her grandmother's expectations.

In the city Mary Lou was truant for 10 out of her 11 school years. Throughout this period, she would travel back and forth between West Virginia and Cincinnati. She repeatedly reenrolled in school in West Virginia only to leave to return to Cincinnati, where she would attend an urban school. At the time she was admitted to the hospital, she was in her junior year. She maintained a straight A average and was on the honor roll. Her peer relationships in school appeared normal, and she was respected by her friends. When she was asked why she felt the need to leave school, she expressed the need to get home for fear something terrible would happen. She felt that "the world was not a safe place, that you simply had to keep a low profile, or something out there would be your downfall." She felt that her strength and her only sense of safety was within her family. Mary Lou also frequently expressed the need to "get away" and would ask her mother to be allowed to go to West Virginia. The mother would oblige.

Mary Lou's mother, like Teresa's, had a difficult time in Cincinnati. She talked about how hard it was for her to leave West Virginia and move to Cincinnati, away from home. Her mother had not made any friends and did not work. Mary Lou became her link with the outside world: she sent Mary Lou to do the grocery shopping and family errands. The mother talked about being transplanted and not yet knowing her way around. While Mary Lou was in the hospital, her mother made frequent phone calls stating that she needed Mary Lou at home. Mary Lou's mother looked to her to act as the parent to her two-year-old. Mary Lou regarded the toddler as a mother would and felt proud when the child reached developmental milestones.

## SUMMARY

In both cases the adolescent girls were expected by their highly problematic and largely dysfunctional mothers to play roles as adults while they were in Cincinnati. In both cases also, livelihood was difficult, albeit in different ways.

In both cases the patients and their families made repeated, often extended, visits to their rural places of origin. The regularity with which Teresa's family returned to Tennessee was related to the absence of kin and to scarce resources in the urban environment. They would travel to Tennessee during the latter part of the month, when their monthly check from AFDC had been depleted. The Tennessee farm, while not large or devoted to cash crops, did raise livestock (pigs) and contain a substantial vegetable garden. People could eat well by consuming both preserved foods and fresh vegetables in season. This was true of Mary Lou in West Virginia as well. Her grandmother would always fix special things for her, and there was always an abundance of food. The rural homeplaces provided temporary residential stability and security, easy communication with the extended family, and a relatively solid economic resource base upon which to draw.

In the case of Mary Lou's mother, the move to Cincinnati had caused her to drop out of the work force to take care of her toddler. This produced isolation for her and dependency upon Mary Lou, who was expected in many ways to replace the role her grandmother had played vis-à-vis her mother in West Virginia. Her grandmother had taken care of Mary Lou while her mother worked. In the city the family became totally dependent upon the wages of Mary Lou's stepfather and felt threatened by their unsafe environment. However, the visits to Tennessee and West Virginia caused real problems for both families. Their efforts to maintain their ties with their extended kin and their attempts to avail themselves of resources (both psychological and economic) in the deep rural areas proved to be very costly. School truancy was exacerbated, and Teresa's mother was unable to work at a job for any length of time, even though she was able to obtain numerous positions.

That Teresa's mother was always unclear as to the length of the visit to the Tennessee homestead is indicative of several complex processes operating in the dynamics of the extended family. These processes include a system of intergenerational reciprocity and one of gender reciprocity (Beaver 1986). Mothers help their daughters when they cannot cope and vice versa. Teresa's grandmother provides food and shelter to her "urban" daughter, and her daughter in turn tries to help her parents when they are ill or when they need other services performed for them, such as help with harvesting and planting. These are conventional expectations. There is pressure to remain in the rural culture because there is always work to be done.

Mary Lou's family was more functional in West Virginia; her mother had a job, and with the grandmother's help, the family could cope with the everyday tasks of providing for the family and caring for children. In the urban setting, Mary Lou takes on the role her grandmother would have played. She shared the role of mother for her sibling with her own mother, just as her mother and grandmother had also shared the parental role for Mary Lou in West Virginia. One wonders how the situation would have been different for Mary Lou and for her mother if the grandmother had moved to Cincinnati with them.

The problem is that the logistics are such that being in two places at the same time is impossible. For Teresa's mother to reenter her extended family and to glean the resources of the farm to supplement her urban wage income proves to be, if not impossible, at least highly problematic. Intergenerational reciprocity does not work when the people live several hundred miles apart.

For the families of Teresa and Mary Lou, the move to the city has meant not prosperity and upward mobility but deprivation and downward mobility. From the point of view of human as well as economic resources, life is much better in the country; there is more living space, more food to eat, and more people for emotional support. The pull of the country is a strong force, both psychologically and economically. For those who refuse to become urban residents, but who want to avail themselves of urban jobs, the shallow rural is one solution. What if Mary Lou's and Teresa's families had moved to the shallow rural instead of the urban area of the region? What would the family structure and the resource base look like?

All migrants to cities do not send their daughters to psychiatric units. Are there any variables that separate Mary Lou's and Teresa's families from other migrants?

People who came from rural Kentucky, West Virginia, and Tennessee in the most recent wave of migration came from the poorest areas and had the most difficult adjustments to make in the city (Schwarzweller and Brown 1970). Borman and Mueninghoff (1983) and Fisher (1976) report that among the 24 parents interviewed in Lower Price Hill, one named 30 relatives living in the neighborhood; only one out of the 24 had no relatives living close by, and most of the respondents named seven or more relatives. Most children in this urban Appalachian neighborhood thus grow up in an environment in which they have sustained interaction with kin who live nearby. Kin are sources of livelihood. Unlike most urban Appalachians in Cincinnati, however, the mothers of the two patients had no kin residing in their neighborhoods. In this respect their families are atypical of urban Appalachians, who tend to relocate near close kin who can provide social and economic support, as well as access to jobs. Therefore, the families of the patients are atypical of migrants in general, who select their urban residences on the basis of where their kin also live.

# ELEVEN

# *Conclusion: Livelihood Processes That Cross Boundaries*

*"In the wild, there are two kinds of cat populations," I tell him when he finishes his move. "Residents and transients. Some stay put, in their fixed home ranges, and others are on the move. They don't have real homes. Everybody always thought that the ones who establish the territories are the most successful—like the capitalists who get ahold of Park Place." (I am eying my opportunities on the board.) "They are the strongest, while the transients are the bums, the losers."*

*"Is that right! I didn't know that." Larry looks genuinely surprised. I think he is surprised at how far the subject itself extends. He is such a specialist. Teeth.*

*I continue bravely. "The thing is—this is what the scientists are wondering about now—it may be that transients are the superior ones after all, with the greatest curiosity and the most intelligence. They can't decide."*

*Mason (1982: 128–129)*

## THE PROBLEM OF BOUNDARIES

Models that pull together the various dimensions of livelihood in a northeastern Kentucky region include different geographical areas, different kinds of economic institutions with different rules for behavior, and different capacities for generating cash, goods, and services.

Whether we are talking specifically about making ends meet the Kentucky way or more generally about the wisdom and logic underlying livelihood processes in other rural parts of the world where people and goods constantly move between agrarian and industrial economies, we are dealing with livelihood processes that cross boundaries: urban and rural, capitalist and noncapitalist, and formal and informal.

Understanding how to think about boundaries and the ways in which they are crossed is absolutely essential for analyzing livelihood processes. The boundary problem is tricky because the boundaries operate in at least two qualitatively different domains: spatial and institutional. The boundaries must be conceived in spatial (geographical) terms, for example, deep rural, shallow rural, and urban. The boundaries must also be understood in institutional (organizational) terms (the kinds of relationships organizing economic processes), for example, capitalist, pre-capitalist, and noncapitalist, formal and informal economies. Both the spatial and the institutional boundaries have accompanying cultural meanings for the people who are moving within and across borders. In short, the analysis concerns a geographical region and the ways in which various institutions organize the economic processes that go on in it. The spatial boundaries refer to geographic entities; the institutional boundaries are more abstract. Both kinds of boundaries, however, require models—special kinds of analytic tools—that can be used to think about the boundaries in both culturally specific and comparative terms. Members of kin networks move through deep rural, shallow rural, and urban areas; they also move in and out of factories, small-scale agrarian units, and marketplaces—different kinds of economies with different principles of organization, relations of production, and work schedules. People are crossing spatial, institutional, and cultural boundaries.

## MODELS FOR GEOGRAPHICAL BOUNDARIES: DEEP RURAL, SHALLOW RURAL, AND URBAN

For the purpose of delineating the geographic space within which people work to "make ends meet," the area under investigation has been defined as a region. The region, however, should not be understood as homogeneous, for it is highly complex and varied. In order to deal with some of the variability in the region—for example, different arrangements of people on the landscape, large and small communities, backroads in some areas and superhighways in others—I have divided the region analytically into three discrete areas: deep rural, shallow rural, and urban. These designations are not folk terms; they should be understood as models with definite empirical referents. Deep rural, shallow rural, and urban are models in the sense that they are ways of dividing up and characterizing the geographical space that exists between what the folk call "the country" and "the city." The division is based on such variables as population density, settlement patterns, and access to infrastructure, primarily roads. For example, deep rural is characterized by lower population densities than either shallow rural or urban. Shallow rural areas have higher population densities than deep rural, but lower population densities than urban areas. Shallow rural is characterized by an elaborate infrastructure not present in the deep rural or in the urban areas. The presence of such an infrastructure in a predominantly rural area in which there is still considerable small-scale agrarian production is what accounts for the remarkable mix of institutions that organize economic activities in the shallow rural. Thus, one finds small farms, factories, and marketplaces all in the shallow rural. But all of these components do not appear simultaneously in the deep rural or urban areas. Again, let me underscore the point that the terms "deep rural," "shallow rural," and "urban" are analytic, not folk, terms. These models allow us to make finer distinctions than would be possible using the common dichotomy: urban versus rural.[1] The spatial models are designed to aid in understanding variability in the accessibility and utilization of the resources and the products of different kinds of economies composed of different institutional arrangements. Theoretically one should be able to identify deep rural, shallow rural, and urban areas all over the world. These concepts are designed to facilitate comparison.

## CROSSING INSTITUTIONAL BOUNDARIES

This study began with a discussion of the problematics of conventional categories. The livelihood processes that are part of the Kentucky way are not easy to pigeonhole. The main reason they are not easy to label or categorize is that they work simultaneously in many different, sometimes conflicting, and often overlapping economic systems: for example, capitalistic labor markets, noncapitalistic marketplaces and agrarian production systems that are combinations of noncapitalist and capitalist systems.[2] Considering the fact that practitioners of the Kentucky way use all of these economies as they move within the region provides a sense of the conceptual and terminological difficulties that have had to be faced in the course of this study. In other words, the economies that work in northeastern Kentucky, what I have for convenience called the agrarian, marketplace, and wage labor economies, are institutionally complex and multifaceted. These economies employ a variety of organizational principles, capitalist and noncapitalist, formal and informal.

## BOUNDARIES OF THE INFORMAL ECONOMY

The problem of understanding the boundaries of the informal economy[3] is growing in importance as more and more people move between different economic sectors. Also, as marketplaces expand, their relationships to the agrarian economy and to the products of the factory system also intensify. Informal economy includes the following: (1) a single or a series of economic processes that operate outside the mainstream economy (in this case, the market, capitalist economy) and (2) that these processes are not recognized by official authorities (in this case, the Internal Revenue Service) as recorded economic transactions. The kinds of economic processes that might be considered formal or informal depend greatly upon the context within which they operate. For example, in Mexico, China, India, and elsewhere in the Third World, marketplace systems traditionally have been the main institutional mechanisms for distributing goods. They are not considered, either by the people or by social scientists, as informal economies.

In northeastern Kentucky the marketing system of rotating periodic marketplaces operates as an informal economy. It is important to understand that the marketplace system would not operate the way it does in this area were it not for the many products of the capitalist system that find their way into the marketplaces—as seconds and as used and old merchandise. The very schedule of the marketplaces themselves is constrained by the wage labor system. Major marketplaces meet on weekends so that wage workers can purchase goods. Wage workers operate booths during their time off from wage work. Buying food in the marketplaces is not the same as buying food in a supermarket. Purchasing watches, household items, and clothing in marketplaces is also very different from purchasing these same items in a shopping mall. While both mainstream and informal economies use cash, in the mainstream economy, prices are determined by price-making markets, for example, the forces of supply and demand in the world economy. This is the market economy.

In contrast, in the informal, marketplace economy, the equivalency rate, or how much of what is exchanged for what, is determined by a number of relationships and factors. Prices in marketplaces (prices are only one form of equivalency) depend in large part on how items are obtained. If goods are bought from a wholesaler, there usually is a minimum price that is determined by price-making markets. However, sellers in marketplaces may decide to use the wholesale price as a ceiling price in the marketplaces. For example, fruits and vegetables obtained from wholesalers will be priced slightly above cost (the wholesale price) at the beginning of a market day. As the day wears on, however, the price of produce goes down, since items are perishable and sellers do not want to transport goods home or discard them. Often, however, people acquire goods for very little money, in auctions and yard sales, for example. Also goods may be acquired for no monetary cost, as gifts from kin or neighbors, or as a result of finding items that have been discarded. Additional labor inputs, such as fixing a broken appliance or mending a broken lamp, will add value to the products sold in marketplaces. Thus, the prices that appear on items in marketplaces may be determined in part by the market system, but are also affected by other forces. Marketplace prices commonly operate below market price and are almost always negotiable. How much sellers are willing to negotiate is based on whether or not the seller perceives the buyer as a "country" or a "city" person. Individual marketplaces also have their own local mechanisms for setting equivalencies. For example, in minor markets the supply and demand of a particular good on a given day will affect its price. Seasonal items or popular items that appear in many booths will have lower marketplace prices. In addition, marketplaces afford opportunities to exchange goods for other goods without using cash. Many market sellers know one another and will negotiate equivalencies.

As I mentioned at the outset, not just one, but several informal economies work to maintain the Kentucky way. The family network itself has many elements of informality. Families organize productive tasks and allocate labor and land within the larger context of a mainstream capitalist economy. They manage to circumvent many of the common constraints of the system. Their work schedules are flexible, although they often work many more than 40 hours per week. Substantial portions of their incomes are not reported to the official tax system. Labor resources seem to move where they are needed to maintain the family network. People use parts of the capitalist economy (often its rejects, seconds, used goods) to their advantage. People also reject and/or resist elements of capitalism by avoiding conspicuous consumption and profiteering of any sort. Practitioners of the Kentucky way go to great lengths to be honest, even to the point that sellers in the marketplaces provide customers with their home phone numbers in case something should need repairs.

Intrafamilial exchanges are often not visible, but they are very much present and important. Members of family networks exchange goods and services regularly without attention to record keeping or reporting. In fact, many economic activities, actual working productive tasks, do not and will not appear anywhere in employment statistics. Odd jobs, for example, usually obtained through kin connections, are aptly named: they exist outside the mainstream economy in the sense that income from them is rarely reported. The nature of their remuneration is a matter of negotiation between two parties; it is in people's best economic interest to treat these jobs as occasional, unimportant, and inconsequential. Such treatment by the folk conceals the actual economic importance of these nonmainstream (informal) work tasks and is a form of resistance to the tax system in particular and capitalism in general.

In the context of the small-scale, subsistence-oriented family farm, kin relations are one set of relations of production. In the deep rural, farm labor is unpaid family labor. Even the cash crops, tobacco, for example, are produced by family members for their own benefit, to purchase necessities. Work tasks are allocated by older family members to other family members. Products of labor (whether food from gardens or cash from tobacco sales) are used by family members for their own maintenance. We see a variation upon this theme in marketplaces.

In addition to the considerable exchanges of labor and goods among kin, there are also some very subtle ways in which kin relations shape decisions about the kinds of economic activities that people choose to pursue. People who work in factories often do so only until someone in their network provides them with another option. What may appear as quitting a job or as irresponsibility toward a job may simply be the replacement of a wage labor job with one or a set of work tasks that are safer, offer better pay and more time flexibility, and provide greater independence and sense of self-worth. Sporadic employment is only sporadic from the viewpoint of one economic sector: the mainstream capitalist economy. People, often young adults, become the subjects of concern when they choose to remain in the temporary wage labor sector to the exclusion of economic activities in the agrarian and/or the marketplace sectors. "Putting all your eggs in one basket" is not considered a wise thing to do.

In sum, the marketplace system interdigitates with kin-based economic units to form a kind of informal economy in northeastern Kentucky. Marketplaces, commonly found in peasant economies throughout the world as the major means of distributing products, are, in this region, alternative economic institutions. They are becoming more and more prominent on the shallow rural landscape. Yet their visibility and prevalence do not reveal the nature of their organization; nor is it immediately apparent what are the linkages between the marketplaces, the agrarian economy, and the factories in the region. Understanding how kin networks operate vis-à-vis marketplaces allows us to unravel the complexities of the system of multiple livelihood strategies.

Many of the members of extended family networks, especially those who sell in the marketplaces, are entrepreneurs. They are not capitalists, however. They are not in business for a profit, or to siphon profits from the labor of hired workers. Rather, they use family labor almost exclusively, and the cash generated from sales of products or from wage labor, in virtually all of the cases, is used to maintain members of the kin network—to provide them with the basic material means necessary for their survival. From the point of view of the people practicing the Kentucky way, cash must be generated for certain purposes: not for accumulation, not for display, but for purchasing those necessities that people cannot produce or obtain in any other way.[4] Selecting jobs that are harmonious with maintaining kin ties is another form of resistance to capitalism.

There is tremendous variability in people's need for cash and in how dependent they are upon it. In part the variability can be accounted for in terms of the extent and character of the family network, its resources, and its geographic accessibility. Cash generation is a maintenance process, just as cash generated in the deep rural was used to "feed the farm." That is, people use cash to maintain the well-being of family members, not for profit. The cash generated by people in the shallow rural as wage workers in factories, or as sellers in marketplaces, is also put back into the family economy in complex, intricate, and subtle ways.[5]

It is not just the maintenance of the household that is at issue in the Kentucky case but the maintenance of the family network itself. Private property provides the base for economic activities aimed toward provisioning and maintenance of family networks (see Gonzalez 1987). Most of the people are not primary producers. That is, while some people certainly sell products that they themselves produce, many of the market vendors are selling both manufactured and recycled goods, as well as reconditioned or used items that they themselves have bought or acquired through exchange.

The importance of the subsistence economy should not be underestimated. All of the family networks have individuals who spend considerable amounts of their time cultivating large gardens and processing food for storage and future consumption. Many people keep livestock as well. All family networks have men and women who hunt, fish, and gather for subsistence purposes. Members of family networks ensure that the products are distributed where they are needed in the network.

The goal of the familial economy is not to ascend the ladder of social stratification. Rather, it is to make ends meet economically and psychologically and to keep the kin network intact through everyday economic activities, many of which have been going on for decades, especially in the agrarian sector. There is a wisdom here—a rationality that has a logic of its own, a steadfastness and a doggedness that has tremendous resiliency, precisely because it is multifaceted and flexible.

The kin network is an umbrella that protects people from depending upon any single economic sector. Here occupation is secondary in defining who people are. The family network, who are "my people," are the critical definers of self and person. The Kentucky way in all of its various forms and manifestations provides people with an identity precisely because it also enables people to make ends meet.[6] Thus, a family imperative guides people's economic activities. Kinship orders livelihood processes that are connected to geographical and residential places (the country, the city, homesteads, and households). These livelihood processes are not bounded by households or by communities. The psychological relationships associated with family and place are expressed by one of Stephen Foster's informants, who suggested that being "at home" in the country means that she need not constantly maneuver to situate herself (1988: 32). In part this means that she could literally stay put and feel comfortable. In the country to be "at home" is also to be at peace psychologically. This psychological connotation is important, especially in light of the adolescents who have been hospitalized because of serious psychiatric disorders. The mothers of these patients grew up in the country but live in the city. The patients and their mothers seem to be maneuvering constantly, but they never manage to become situated. Both mothers and daughters are shifting both geographically (from country to city in a bilocal residence pattern) and psychologically (mothers exhibit resistance to taking on adult roles and their daughters suffer the consequences). Their extended visits to the country render both mothers and daughters unsettled, transients in both the country and the city. The temporary quality of their lives and the ambivalence expressed, particularly by the mothers, to both country and city, create a situation to which their adolescent daughters cannot adapt. To say this in different terms, their kin network became stretched to the breaking point. Because of the geographical distance between country and city, the normal intergenerational ties between mothers, grandmothers (in the country) and daughters, now mothers (in the city) cannot be maintained. The mothers in the city need their mothers to help with child care and with general family maintenance, economic and psychological. An important part of the support and maintenance is, of course, economic. In the city, people become cash dependent, but there is not enough cash to make ends meet. Thus, numerous trips to the country become necessary and create a vicious cycle of ambivalence. Without the economic and the psychological support, the women could not function normally in the city as mothers for their adolescent daughters.

The shallow rural seems to provide a sense of place for people. If people maintain a land base, the shallow rural functions both economically and psychologically like the country. It can be a rural place of residence. It is in this sense that many people in the shallow rural do not have to maneuver psychologically.[7]

## RESISTANCE AND THE LIVELIHOOD OF KIN

*When a peasant hides part of his crop to avoid paying taxes, he is both filling his stomach and depriving the state of grain. When a peasant soldier deserts the army because the food is bad and his crops at home are ripe, he is both looking after himself and denying the state cannon fodder. When such acts are rare and isolated, they are of little interest; but when they become a consistent pattern (even though uncoordinated, let alone organized) we are dealing with resistance. The intrinsic nature and, in one sense, the "beauty" of much peasant resistance is that it often confers immediate and concrete advantages, while at the same time denying re- sources to the appropriating classes, and that it requires little or no mani- fest organization. The stubbornness and force of such resistance flow directly from the fact that it is so firmly rooted in the shared material struggle experienced by a class. . . . "Bread and butter" issues are the es- sence of lower-class politics and resistance. Consumption, from this per- spective, is both the goal and the result of resistance and counterresistance.*

*Scott (1985:295–296)*

Making ends meet in rural agrarian economies is not a simple matter. We can think of peasant societies as rural societies in which all eco- nomic activities at the local and regional levels, including those orga- nized by kin networks, are affected by contact with the nation-state (Wolf 1966).[8] The Kentucky way fits into this definition of peasant econo- mies, even though the word "peasant" carries a negative connotation in rural America. The concept of peasantry is intermediate in both a spa- tial and economic sense. If we realize that nation-states exist in larger world economic systems, then virtually every aspect of the rural econ- omy is touched, in some way, by state bureaucracies and world markets. From the vantage point of national and regional elites, peasants may be regarded as a class of agrarian producers (Halperin 1977a:12). These agrarian producers constitute the labor force for the market economy, a labor force that must be maintained and reproduced. Rural agrarian so- cieties in state systems cannot be thought of as isolated entities; they must be considered as integral parts of industrial capitalism.

The strategies treated in this study can be understood as forms of re- sistance to capitalism and of dependency upon the state (Comaroff 1985). The multiple livelihood strategies that are organized by family networks—by practicing the Kentucky way—in this Appalachian re- gion are indeed organized. That this organization may not be apparent is in part a function of the family's dispersement on the regional land- scape. The informal nature of the cash-generating strategies renders their structure hidden to the casual, and even the not so casual, ob- server. Flea markets appear as observable phenomena but not imme- diately as parts of a structured system of rotating periodic marketplaces. The fact that the marketplaces are only one piece of a complex system of livelihood strategies is also not immediately obvious.

Marketplaces are public, open arenas with private, hidden agendas. People use the system very carefully: they plan their movements; they calculate a whole series of variables into their buying patterns, their selling locations, and the timing of both. The behaviors of individuals— those who quit their temporary wage labor jobs, or who refuse to continue to work for a painting contractor or the Salvation Army—do not appear immediately to belong to a structured system of extended family relationships that ensures the circulation of goods and services. A mother's or a father's few moments of conversation with a wage laborer son, who literally passes through a marketplace, can coordinate a large family gathering during which food, information, goods, and services are exchanged. Even if no gathering is planned, people can check in at designated times and at designated places to plan a whole series of activities, to coordinate transportation of goods from one place to another, to distribute food, and so forth. These coordination processes are forms of control that enable people to resist becoming dependent upon the capitalist economy.

Just before Christmas 1986, a woman I met at an auction told me that she and her husband went for five months with no income. When I asked her how they managed to make ends meet, she told me, "We trusted in the Lord." The husband had retired from a wage labor job at the age of 42. Several heart attacks and an operation had placed him on disability. She told me that they were glad they had their house paid for and that they have "a little farm" of 10 acres and a garden. She was expecting her three daughters and five grandchildren for Christmas dinner. After Christmas she and her sister will resume their selling at the Redside Market. "We laugh and look around," she said.

Forms of resistance to capitalism, to dependence upon cash from wage labor are subtle. Often they are hidden and, as a consequence, all the more powerful. The failure of "country people" to talk to "city people," the stares at the auctions, the covert hostility to outsiders. These are not merely manifestations of fears of the tax collector, but resistance to invasions of privacy—the privacy to create alternative forms of livelihood.

# The Vendor Population at the Redside Market: A Sample

The data presented in this section illustrate some of the key characteristics of the vendor population at the Redside Market, the most important of the major markets in the shallow rural sector of the region. The largest and the most centrally located of the major markets, it is the one we studied most intensively. The sample is representative of all booths in the market, with the exception of the ones that are permanent, storelike booths. It is based upon data collected on five market days, ranging seasonally from early spring to midsummer. The total number of sellers included is 411, and the total number of booths is 294.

All booths were canvassed for the age and sex of the sellers. The presence of one, two, or three generations was also counted.

## AGE

The ages given in the following tables are estimates. Table A.1 shows the age distribution of sellers at the Redside Market. The majority of the selling population is between the ages of 30 and 49, but all ages are represented. The median age is 35.66 years, a figure somewhat higher than the median age of residents in the northern Kentucky region, which is 29.1 years of age (1980 census).

The number of sellers in upper age categories (especially 40+) is indicative of the importance of intergenerational ties in the marketplace as a whole. In order to document the extent of cross-generational ties, we have calculated the number of booths with at least two generations present. These figures are also estimates. From these cases we can see that often the intergenerational ties that bear upon marketplace activities are invisible. People may participate in production for the marketplace; they may provide child care for the sellers or help with the acquisition of goods. These people may or may not be physically present in the

**TABLE A.1**
**Frequency of Males and Females by Age Range for**
**Five Market Days (April–July)**

| Age Range | Males | Females | Total |
|-----------|-------|---------|-------|
| 0–9       | 7     | 5       | 12    |
| 10–19     | 38    | 34      | 72    |
| 20–29     | 26    | 37      | 63    |
| 30–39     | 47    | 48      | 95    |
| 40–49     | 54    | 41      | 95    |
| 50–59     | 23    | 18      | 41    |
| 60+       | 16    | 17      | 33    |
| Total     | 211   | 200     | 411   |

booths on market days. Table A.2 shows the number of booths in the Redside sample in which two or three generations are visible.

## GENDER

The Redside sample suggests that marketplace vending is a task shared equally by the sexes. The average percentage of marketers who are male is 51.34 percent, and 48.66 percent are female. Comparing the frequencies of males and females in Table A.1 highlights the importance of position in the life course. Males are less prominent as marketplace vendors from the ages of 20 to 29 than are females (see Table A.3 for percentages). At this point in the life course, many men are heavily involved in the wage labor economy. We must be careful here, however, since the absence of young adult men in the marketplace does not indicate total noninvolvement. The son of Ester and Walter, for example, is a truck driver who checks up on his parents in the Redside Market. We can say, however, that these men probably function as consumers of marketplace goods. Males outnumber females in the 40–50 age range, however. In fact, male participation in marketplaces appears to peak at this age range. How to explain this difference is difficult. Do males begin to be laid off from wage labor jobs between the ages of 40 and 50? If so, then market selling becomes an alternative cash-generating strategy for males of this age range.

## TABLE A.2
## Intergenerational Cooperation in Booths at Redside Market

| Observa-tional Dates | Intergenerational Booths | | | | | | Total Booths |
|---|---|---|---|---|---|---|---|
| | 2 Generations | | 3 Generations | | Total | | |
| | N | % | N | % | N | % | |
| 4/12/86 | 2 | 10.5 | 2 | 10.5 | 4 | 21.1 | 19 |
| 4/20/86 | 6 | 11.3 | 2 | 3.8 | 8 | 15.1 | 53 |
| 4/27/86 | 12 | 17.9 | 1 | 1.5 | 13 | 19.4 | 67 |
| 5/17/86 | 10 | 13.2 | 4 | 5.3 | 14 | 13.4 | 76 |
| 7/6/86 | 5 | 6.3 | 2 | 2.5 | 7 | 8.9 | 79 |
| Average (Mean) | 7.0 | 11.9 | 2.2 | 3.7 | 9.2 | 15.6 | 58.8 |

## TABLE A.3
## Percentage of Males and Females by Age Range for Five Market Days (April–July)

| Age Range | Males | Females | Total |
|---|---|---|---|
| 0–9 | 3.3 | 2.5 | 2.9 |
| 10–19 | 18.0 | 17.0 | 17.5 |
| 20–29 | 12.3 | 18.5 | 15.3 |
| 30–39 | 22.2 | 24.0 | 23.1 |
| 40–49 | 25.6 | 20.5 | 23.1 |
| 50–59 | 10.9 | 9.0 | 10.0 |
| 60+ | 7.6 | 8.5 | 8.0 |
| Total | 99.9 | 100 | 99.9 |

# *Notes*

## 1. Introduction

1. Segalen and Zonabend (1987:112–114) note the necessity of devising an adequate conceptual terminology and vocabulary to keep abreast of developments in the anthropology of kinship in European societies. They also note the problem of "the role of economics as it connects with kinship or becomes autonomous from it. In peasant societies, especially, where the way of life is linked to access to land, the system of land tenure and farm ownership, price and market conditions must be known both independently from the facts of kinship and also in their relationship with kinship" (1987:113).

2. The field of economic anthropology is large and full of controversy. For some standard works, see my *Economies across Cultures* (1988); the series Research in Economic Anthropology, edited by Barry L. Isaac (1984 to the present); and the proceedings of the Society for Economic Anthropology, especially Ortiz (1983). See also Gudeman (1986), Godelier (1966, 1986), Dalton (1961, 1968, 1969, 1971, 1972), Cook (1973), Halperin and Dow (1977), LeClair and Schneider (1967), Pryor (1977), Plattner (1975), Belshaw (1965), and Bohannan and Bohannan (1968).

## 2. An Overview

1. It is important to realize that even the most isolated communities in the Appalachian region have been tied to national and international economies for well over a century. For example, ginseng, a plant used by the Chinese for medicinal purposes, has been exported from Appalachian communities to Chinese communities in New York since the nineteenth century (Hicks 1976).

2. See chapters 7 and 11 for a more extended discussion of the concepts "market," "marketplace," and "market system."

3. Judith Ennew says that for the Hebrides crofting provides an occupational baseline, a continuity within a shifting employment pattern. She points to the strong ideological associations of agriculture, even though the agricultural aspects of crofting are not a major component of occupational pluralism (1980:57).

4. For a discussion of regional analysis and its comparative potentials, see Smith (1976a, 1976b, 1983, 1985).

5. For comparative material, see Nutini and Murphy (1968), who argue that, for the Tlaxcala-Pueblan area of Mexico, labor migration is related to a strengthening of kinship obligations.

6. For comparative material on the rural origins of the Swedish working class, see Löfgren (1987).

7. See West's (1945) study of Plainville, Hicks (1976), and Beaver (1986). Much of this literature is reviewed in chapter 3.

## 4. Historical and Anthropological Overview

1. I do not want to suggest that Appalachian ethnicity is entirely homogeneous. See Turner (1985) and Perdue (1979).

2. For further discussion of noncapitalist and precapitalist economic formations, the following works should be consulted: Chayanov (1966), Kahn and Llobera (1981), Taussig (1980), Godelier (1976), and Marx (1971).

## 5. Deep Rural Economy

1. One of the reasons it is possible to produce tobacco as the major source of cash is precisely because labor costs are practically free. Meals must be provided for workers, however. In Beech Creek in 1942, relatively small amounts of cash were earned from small tobacco acreages. Burley tobacco was the only major cash crop, and no farmer produced more than 1.5 acres. This accounted for about 35 percent of the total cash income from farm products. Additional cash income came from egg and livestock sales (Schwarzweller, Brown, and Mangalem 1971:6).

## 6. Multiple Livelihood Strategies in the Shallow Rural Area

1. It should be emphasized that people traditionally have expected layoffs and have planned for them. That is, they have never viewed jobs in the wage labor sector as reliable or secure. The shift from wage labor to odd jobs and agrarian production is part of the overall livelihood strategy.

## 10. The Breakdown of Multiple Livelihood Strategies

1. For a discussion of the psychiatric and cultural implications of the case histories, see Halperin and Slomowitz 1988.

## 11. Conclusion

1. The development of the subfield urban anthropology has dealt with urban-rural relationships. With a few exceptions, it has accentuated the rural urban dichotomy while pointing out the class commonalities that override the distinction. See Swetnam (1978); Hunt and Hunt (1968); Weisner (1976). See also Giddens (1979) on structure and agency and Bourdieu (1977).

2. For a discussion of linkages between formal and informal sectors of the economy, see Trager (1985) and Lomnitz (1988).

3. The term *urban informal sector,* or informal economy, was first used by Keith Hart (1973) to identify a set of income-earning opportunities in Ghana.

There has been a virtual explosion of discussion of informal economies over the last several years (Gerry 1987; Grossman 1988; Gaughan and Ferman 1987; Halperin and Sturdevant 1988).

4. Henretta (1978:30) writes that farm families usually trained and encouraged their children to "succeed *them* rather than to 'succeed' by rising in the social system."

5. Cook and Diskin (1976) point out that in the Oaxaca economy a large majority of producer-sellers (*propios*) and middlemen-traders (*regatones*) "expend time and labor in the production of use and exchange values destined to the provisioning and maintenance of their household units, and not to the expansion of their business assets in a systematic, cumulative way. . . . Exchange values are sought and acquired by these 'peasant' actors (most of them do cultivate the soil for subsistence purposes) as indirect means to acquire use values produced by others; they do not seek them as direct means to accrue profits for reinvestment in profit-making enterprises. This is, then, production and exchange embedded in a process of petty commodity circulation, where maintenance of the household unit (i.e., funding of subsistence, rent, capital re-accumulation, and ceremonial needs) is the rule, and expansion of business activities is the exception" (1976:135).

6. For comparative materials, see Cohen (1978, 1979, 1982a, 1982b, 1985), Kertzer (1984), Plakans (1977). See also articles in Appadurai (1986).

7. Nutini and Murphy (1968:83) note that income from peasant's farm crops provides the labor migrant with an important means of both psychological and economic security. Elkan (1960:134–135) also points to the rural farming component of urban migrant's income in Uganda.

8. The literature on European peasants is particularly noteworthy for its comparative potential (see Lofgren 1980; Cole and Wolf 1974). Latin American peasantries also add to comparative analysis (Stein 1975; Nutini and Isaac 1974).

# Bibliography

Alexander, Frank D., and Robert E. Galloway
  1947   "Salient Features of Social Organization in a Typical County of
          the General and Self-Sufficient Farm Region." *Rural Sociology* 12:
          395–405.
Appadurai, Arjun, ed.
  1986   *The Social Life of Things: Commodities in Cultural Perspective.*
          Cambridge: Cambridge University Press.
Arcury, Thomas
  1984   "Household Composition and Economic Change in a Rural Commu-
          nity, 1900–1980: Testing Two Models." *American Ethnologist* 11:
          677–698.
Arensberg, Conrad
  1937   *The Irish Countryman.* New York: Peter Smith.
Axton, W. F.
  1975   *Tobacco and Kentucky.* Lexington: University Press of Kentucky.
Ball, Richard A.
  1968   "A Poverty Case: The Analgesic Subculture of the Southern Ap-
          palachians." *American Sociological Review* 33:885–895.
Banks, Alan J.
  1980   "The Emergence of a Capitalistic Labor Market in Eastern Ken-
          tucky." *Appalachian Journal* 7:175–190.
Batteau, Alan
  1982a  "The Contradictions of a Kinship Community." In *Holding on to the
          Land and the Lord,* ed. Robert L. Hall and Carol B. Stack. Athens:
          University of Georgia Press.
  1982b  "Mosbys and Broomsedge: The Semantics of Class in an Appalachian
          Kinship System." *American Ethnologist* 9:445–466.
Batteau, Alan, ed.
  1983   *Appalachia and America: Autonomy and Regional Dependence.*
          Lexington: University Press of Kentucky.

Beals, Ralph L.
   1970    "Gifting, Reciprocity, Savings, and Credit in Peasant Oaxaca." *South-*
           *western Journal of Anthropology* 26.3:231–241.
   1975    *The Peasant Marketing System of Oaxaca, Mexico.* Berkeley and Los
           Angeles: University of California Press.
   1976    "Oaxaca Market Study Project: Origins, Scope, and Preliminary Find-
           ings." In *Markets in Oaxaca,* ed. Scott Cook and Martin Diskin. Aus-
           tin: University of Texas Press.
Beaver, Patricia D.
   1986    *Rural Community in the Appalachian South.* Lexington: University
           Press of Kentucky.
Belshaw, Cyril S.
   1965    *Traditional Exchange and Modern Markets.* Englewood Cliffs, N.J.:
           Prentice-Hall.
Berry, Wendel
   1985    *Nathan Coulter.* Boston: Houghton Mifflin.
Billings, Dwight, Kathleen Blee, and Louis Swanson
   1986    "Culture, Family, and Community in Preindustrial Appalachia." *Ap-*
           *palachian Journal* 13:154–170.
Bohannan, Paul, and Laura Bohannan
   1968    *Tiv Economy.* Evanston: Northwestern University Press.
Borman, Kathryn, and Elaine Mueninghoff
   1983    "Lower Price Hill's Children." In *Appalachia and America: Auton-*
           *omy and Regional Dependence,* ed. Alan Batteau. Lexington: Uni-
           versity Press of Kentucky.
Bott, Elizabeth
   1957    *Family and Social Network.* London: Tavistock Publications.
Bourdieu, Pierre
   1977    *Outline of a Theory of Practice.* Cambridge: Cambridge University
           Press.
Brody, Eugene B., ed.
   1970    *Behavior in New Environments: Adaptation of Migrant Populations.*
           Beverly Hills: Sage Publications.
Brown, James S.
   1952    *The Family Group in a Kentucky Mountain Farming Community.*
           Agricultural Experiment Station Bulletin 588. Lexington: University
           of Kentucky.
Bryant, Carlene
   1979    "We're All Kin: A Cultural Study of an East Tennessee Mountain
           Neighborhood." Ph.D. diss., Cornell University.
   1981    *We're All Kin: A Cultural Study of an East Tennessee Mountain*
           *Neighborhood.* Knoxville: University of Tennessee Press.
   1983    "Family Group Organization in a Cumberland Mountain Neighbor-
           hood." In *Appalachia and America: Autonomy and Regional Depen-*
           *dence,* ed. Alan Batteau. Lexington: University Press of Kentucky.

Calnek, F. P.
 1978 "El Sistema de Mercado en Tenochtitlán." In *Economía Política e Ideología en el México Prehispánico,* ed. Pedro Carrasco and Johanna Broda. Mexico City: Nueva Imagen for CIS-INAH.
Carraco, Dan
 1987 "Burley Tobacco." *Journal of Kentucky Studies,* pp. 12–21.
Caudill, Harry M.
 1962 *Night Comes to the Cumberlands.* Boston: Little, Brown.
 1971 *My Land Is Dying.* New York: Dutton.
 1976 *Watches of the Night.* Boston: Atlantic–Little, Brown.
Chapman, Anne
 1957 "Port of Trade Enclaves in Aztec and Maya Civilizations." In *Trade and Markets in the Early Empires,* ed. Karl Polanyi, Conrad Arensberg, and Harry W. Pearson. Glencoe, Ill.: Free Press.
Chayanov, Aleksandr V.
 1966 *Chayanov on the Theory of Peasant Economy.* Edited by Daniel Thorner, Basile Kerblay, and R. E. F. Smith. Homewood, Ill.: Richard D. Irwin for the American Economic Association (originally published 1925).
Cohen, Anthony
 1978 "'The Same—But Different': The Allocation of Identity in Whalsay, Shetland." *Sociological Review* 26.3:449–470.
 1979 "The Whalsay Croft: Traditional Work and Customary Identity in Modern Times." In *Social Anthropology of Work,* ed. Sandra Wallman. New York: Academic Press.
 1982a "Blockade: A Case Study of Local Consciousness in an Extra-Local Event." In *Belonging: Identity and Social Organization in British Rural Cultures,* ed. A. Cohen. Manchester: Manchester University Press.
 1982b "A Sense of Time, A Sense of Place: The Meaning of Close Association in Whalsay, Shetland." In *Belonging: Identity and Social Organization in British Rural Cultures,* ed. A. Cohen. Manchester: Manchester University Press.
 1985 "Symbolism and Social Change: Matters of Life and Death in Whalsay, Shetland." *Man* 20.2:307–324.
Cole, John W., and Eric R. Wolf
 1974 *The Hidden Frontier: Ecology and Ethnicity in the Alpine Valley.* New York: Academic Press.
Coles, Robert
 1971 *Migrants, Sharecroppers, and Mountaineers.* Boston: Atlantic–Little, Brown.
Coles, Robert, and Jane H. Coles
 1978 *Women of Crisis: Lives of Struggle and Hope.* New York: Delacourt Press.
Comaroff, Jean
 1985 *Body of Power, Spirit of Resistance: The Culture and History of a South African People.* Chicago: University of Chicago Press.

Cook, Scott

1973 "Economic Anthropology: Problems in Theory, Method, and Analysis." In *Handbook of Social and Cultural Anthropology*, ed. John J. Honigman. Chicago: Rand McNally.

1976 "The 'Market' as Location and Transaction: Dimensions of Marketing in a Zapote Stoneworking Industry." In *Markets in Oaxaca*, ed. Scott Cook and Martin Diskin. Austin: University of Texas Press.

Cook, Scott, and Martin Diskin, eds.

1976 *Markets in Oaxaca.* Austin: University of Texas Press.

Dalton, George

1961 "Economic Theory and Primitive Society." *American Anthropologist* 63:1–25.

1968 Introduction. In *Primitive, Archaic, and Modern Economies: Essays of Karl Polanyi.* Edited by George Dalton. Garden City, N.Y.: Doubleday-Anchor.

1969 "Theoretical Issues in Economic Anthropology." *Current Anthropology* 10:63–102.

1971 *Studies in Economic Anthropology.* Washington, D.C.: American Anthropological Association.

1972 "Peasantries in Anthropology and History." *Current Anthropology* 13:385–497.

Danna, J. J.

1980 "Migration and Mental Illness: What Role Do Traditional Childhood Socialization Practices Play?" *Culture, Medicine, and Psychiatry* 4:25–42.

Day, Kay Young

1982 "Kinship in a Changing Economy: A View from the Sea Islands." In *Holding on to the Land and the Lord*, ed. Robert L. Hall and Carol B. Stack. Athens: University of Georgia Press.

Diskin, Martin

1969 "Estudio Estructural del Sistema de Plaza en el Valle de Oaxaca." *América Indígena* 29:1077–1099.

1976 "Peasant Market System Structure." In *Markets in Oaxaca*, ed. Scott Cook and Martin Diskin. Austin: University of Texas Press.

Eder, Herbert M.

1976 "Markets as Mirrors: Reflections of the Economic Activity and the Regional Culture of Coastal Oaxaca." In *Markets in Oaxaca*, ed. Scott Cook and Martin Diskin. Austin: University of Texas Press.

Elder, Glen H.

1981 "History and the Family: The Discovery of Complexity." *Journal of Marriage and the Family* 43:489–519.

Elkan, Walter

1960 *Migrants and Proletarians: Urban Labor in the Economic Development of Uganda.* London: Oxford University Press.

Eller, Ronald

1982 *Miners, Millhands, and Mountaineers: Industrialization of the Appalachian South, 1880–1930.* Knoxville: University of Tennessee Press.

Ennew, Judith
    1980    *The Western Isles Today.* Cambridge: Cambridge University Press.
Fisher, Stephen L.
    1976    "Victim Blaming in Appalachia: Cultural Theories and the Southern Mountaineer." In *Appalachia: Social Context Past and Present,* 2d ed., ed. Bruce Ergood and Bruce E. Kuhre. Dubuque, Iowa: Kendall/Hunt.
Foster, George M.
    1948    "The Folk Economy of Rural Mexico, with Special Reference to Marketing." *Journal of Marketing* 13:153–162.
Foster, Stephen William
    1977    "Identity as Symbolic Production: The Politics of Culture and Meaning in Appalachia." Ph.D. diss., Princeton University.
    1988    *The Past Is Another Country.* Berkeley and Los Angeles: University of California Press.
Gaughan, Joseph P., and Louis A. Ferman
    1987    "Toward an Understanding of the Informal Economy. In *The Informal Economy,* ed. Louis A. Ferman, Stuart Henry, and Michele Hoyman. Beverly Hills: Sage Publications.
Gaventa, John
    1980    *Power and Powerlessness: Quiescence and Rebellion in an Appalachian Valley.* Urbana: University of Illinois Press.
Geertz, Clifford
    1963    *Peddlers and Princes: Social Development and Economic Change in Two Indonesian Towns.* Chicago: University of Chicago Press.
    1979    "Suq: The Bazaar Economy in Sefron." In *Meaning and Order in Moroccan Society,* ed. Clifford Geertz, Hildred Geertz, and L. Rosen. Cambridge: Cambridge University Press.
    1983    *Local Knowledge: Further Essays in Interpretive Anthropology.* New York: Basic Books.
Gerry, Chris
    1987    "Developing Economies and the Informal Sector in Historical Perspective." In *The Informal Economy,* ed. Louis A. Ferman, Stuart Henry, and Michele Hoyman. Beverly Hills: Sage Publications.
Giardina, Denise
    1987    *Storming Heaven.* New York: Ballantine Books.
Giddens, Anthony
    1979    *Central Problems in Social Theory.* Berkeley and Los Angeles: University of California Press.
Godelier, Maurice
    1966    *Rationality and Irrationality in Economics.* New York: Monthly Review Press.
    1976    *Perspectives in Marxist Anthropology.* Cambridge: Cambridge University Press.
    1986    *The Mental and the Material: Thought, Economy, and Society.* Translated by Martin Thom. London: Routledge, Chapman & Hall.

Gonzalez, Nancie S.
    1969    *Black Carib Household Structure.* Seattle: University of Washington Press.
    1987    Family Lab
Goody, Jack
    1972    "The Evolution of the Family." In *Household and Family in Past Time,* ed. Peter Lasslet and Richard Wall. Cambridge: Cambridge University Press.
    1976    *Production and Reproduction.* Cambridge: Cambridge University Press.
Goody, Jack, ed.
    1958    *The Development Cycle in Domestic Groups.* Cambridge: Cambridge University Press.
Greenfield, Sidney, and Arnold Strickon
    1986    *Entrepreneurship and Social Change.* Monographs in Economic Anthropology No. 2. Lanham, Md.: University Press of America.
Grossman, Gregory, ed.
    1988    *Studies in the Second Economy of Communist Countries.* Berkeley and Los Angeles: University of California Press.
Gudeman, Stephen
    1986    *Economics as Culture: Models and Metaphors of Livelihood.* London: Routledge and Kegan Paul.
Hall, Robert L., and Carol B. Stack, eds.
    1982    *Holding on to the Land and the Lord: Kinship, Ritual, Land Tenure, and Social Policy in the Rural South.* Athens: University of Georgia Press.
Halperin, Rhoda
    1977    "Conclusion: A Substantive Approach to Peasant Livelihood." In *Peasant Livelihood: Studies in Economic Anthropology and Cultural Ecology,* ed. Rhoda Halperin and James Dow. New York: St. Martin's Press.
    1988    *Economies across Cultures.* London: Macmillan.
    1991    "Polanyi's Concept of Householding: Resistance and the Livelihood of Kin in an Appalachian Region." In *Research in Economic Anthropology* 13, ed. Barry Isaac. Greenwich, Conn.: JAI Press. Forthcoming.
Halperin, Rhoda, and James Dow
    1977    *Peasant Livelihood: Studies in Economic Anthropology and Cultural Ecology.* New York: St. Martin's Press.
Halperin, Rhoda, and Marcia Slomowitz
    1988    "Hospitalized Appalachian Adolescents." In *Appalachian Mental Health,* ed. Susan Keefe. Lexington: University Press of Kentucky.
Halperin, Rhoda, and Sara Sturdevant
    1988    "A Cross-Cultural Treatment of the Informal Economy." Paper presented at the Society for Economic Anthropology, Knoxville, Tenn.
Hammel, Eugene A.
    1972    "The Zadruga as Process." In *Household and Family in Past Time,*

ed. Peter Laslett and Richard Wall. Cambridge: Cambridge University Press.

Hart, Keith
1973    "Informal Income Opportunities and Urban Employment in Ghana." *Journal of Modern African Studies* 11:61–89.

Heller, Peter L., and Gustavo Quesada
1977    "Rural Familism: An Interregional Analysis." *Rural Sociology* 42: 220–240.

Henretta, James A.
1978    "Families and Farms: Mentality in Pre-Industrial America." *William and Mary Quarterly*, pp. 3–32.

Hicks, George L.
1976    *Appalachian Valley.* New York: Holt, Rinehart and Winston.

Higgs, Robert J., and Ambrose N. Manning, eds.
1975    *Voices from the Hills: Selected Readings from Southern Appalachia.* New York: Ungar.

Hill, Polly
1966    "Notes on Traditional Market Authority and Market Periodicity in West Africa." *Journal of African History* 2.2:295–311.

Holmes, Douglas R.
1983    "A Peasant-Worker Model in a Northern Italian Context." *American Ethnologist* 10:734–748.

Holmes, Douglas R., and Jean H. Quataert
1986    "An Approach to Modern Labor: Worker Peasantries in Historic Saxony and the Friuli Region over Three Centuries." *Comparative Study of Society and History* 28:191–216.

Hunt, Eva, and Robert Hunt
1968    "The Role of Courts in Rural Mexico." In *Peasants in the Modern World*, ed. Philip Bock. Albuquerque: University of New Mexico Press.

Isaac, Barry L.
1984    Introduction. In *Research in Economic Anthropology.* Vol. 6. Greenwich, Conn.: JAI Press.

Jackson, Anthony
1987    "Reflections on Ethnography at Home and the ASA." In *Anthropology at Home*, ed. Anthony Jackson. London: Tavistock Publications.

Kahn, Kathy
1973    *Hillbilly Women.* New York: Doubleday.

Kahn, Joel, and Josep Llobera
1981    "Towards a New Marxism or a New Anthropology?" In *The Anthropology of Precapitalist Societies.* London: Macmillan.

Kaplan, Berton H.
1971    *Blue Ridge: An Appalachian Community in Transition.* Morgantown: Office of Research and Development, Appalachian Center, West Virginia University.

Kaplan, David
    1965   "The Mexican Marketplace Then and Now." *Proceedings of the 1965 Annual Spring Meeting of the American Ethnological Society.* Seattle: University of Washington Press.

Keefe, Susan Emley
    1988   *Appalachian Mental Health.* Lexington: University Press of Kentucky.

Kertzer, David
    1984   "Anthropology and Family History." *Journal of Family History* 9: 210–216.

Kingsolver, Barbara
    1988   *The Bean Trees.* New York: Harper and Row.

Laslett, Peter
    1972   "The History of the Family." In *Household and Family in the Past Time,* ed. Peter Laslett and Richard Wall. Cambridge: Cambridge University Press.

Leacock, Eleanor B., ed.
    1970   *The Culture of Poverty: A Critique.* New York: Simon and Schuster.

LeClair, Edward E., Jr., and Harold N. Schneider
    1968   *Economic Anthropology: Readings in Theory and Analysis.* New York: Holt, Rinehart and Winston.

Lewis, Helen Matthews
    1978   "The Colony of Appalachia." In *Colonialism in Modern America: The Appalachian Case,* ed. Helen Matthews Lewis, Linda Johnson, and Donald Askins. Boone, N.C.: Appalachian Consortium Press.

Lofgren, Orvar
    1980   "Historical Perspectives on Scandinavian Peasantries." *Annual Review of Anthropology* 9: 187–314.
    1987   "Deconstructing Swedishness: Culture and Class in Modern Sweden." In *Anthropology at Home,* ed. Anthony Jackson. London: Tavistock Publications.

Lomnitz, Larissa A.
    1988   "Informal Sector, Petty Commodity Production, and the Social Relations of Small-Scale Enterprise." In *The New Economic Anthropology,* ed. John Clammer. New York: St. Martin's Press.

Looff, David H.
    1971   *Appalachia's Children: The Challenge of Mental Health.* Lexington: University Press of Kentucky.

Maclachlan, Morgan D.
    1987   *Household Economies and Their Transformations.* New York: University Press of America.

Malinowski, Bronislaw, and Julio de la Fuente
    1957   "La Economía de un Sistema de Mercados en México: Un Ensayo de Etnografía Contemporánea y Cambio Social en un Valle Mexicano. *Acta Antropología.* (Mexico City) 1.2: 14–31.

Marroquin, Alejandro
1957 *La Ciudad Mercado: Tlaxiaco, Mexico.* Mexico City: Instituto Indigenista, Imprenta Universitaria.
Marx, Karl
1973 *Grundrisse: Foundations of the Critique of Political Economy.* New York: Vintage Books (originally published 1939).
Mason, Bobbie Ann
1982 *Shiloh and Other Stories.* New York: Harper and Row.
1989 *Love Life.* New York: Harper and Row.
McCoy, Clyde B., and James S. Brown
1981 "Appalachian Migration to Midwestern Cities." In *The Invisible Minority: Urban Appalachians,* ed. William W. Philliber and Clyde B. McCoy. Lexington: University Press of Kentucky.
McCoy, Clyde B., and Virginia Watkins
1981 "Stereotypes of Appalachian Migrants." In *The Invisible Minority: Urban Appalachians,* ed. William W. Philliber and Clyde B. McCoy. Lexington: University Press of Kentucky.
Minge-Kalman, Wanda
1978 "Household Economy during the Peasant-to-Worker Transition in the Swiss Alps." *Ethnology* 17.2:183−97.
Montell, William L.
1986 *Killings: Folk Justice in the Upper South.* Lexington: University Press of Kentucky.
Netting, Robert M., Richard R. Wilk, and Eric J. Arnould, eds.
1984 *Household: Comparative and Historical Studies of the Domestic Group.* Berkeley and Los Angeles: University of California Press.
Newby, Howard
1978 *Property, Paternalism, and Power.* London: Hutchison.
Norman, Gurney
1977 *Kinfolks: The Wilgus Stories.* Frankfort, Ky.: Gnomon Press.
Nutini, Hugo, and Barry L. Isaac
1974 *Los Pueblos de Habla Nahuatl de la Región de Tlaxcala y Puebla.* Mexico City: Instituto Nacional Indigenista.
Nutini, Hugo, and Tim Murphy
1968 "Labor Migration and Family Structure in the Tlaxcala-Pueblan Area, Mexico." In *Essays in Honor of Ralph Beals,* ed. Walter Goldschmidt. Berkeley and Los Angeles: University of California Press.
Obermiller, Phillip J.
1981 "The Question of Appalachian Ethnicity." In *The Invisible Minority: Urban Appalachians,* ed. William M. Philliber and Clyde B. McCoy. Lexington: University Press of Kentucky.
Opie, John
1977 "A Sense of Place." In *An Appalachian Symposium,* ed. J. W. Williamson. Boone, N. C.: Appalachian State University Press.

Ortiz, Sutti
    1967    "Columbian Rural Market Organization: An Exploratory Model."
            *Man* 2.3 : 393–413.
    1983    "What Is Decision Analysis About? The Problem of Formal Repre-
            sentations." In *Economic Anthropology: Topics and Theories,* ed.
            Sutti Ortiz. Lanham, Md.: University Press of America.
Pappas, Gregory
    1989    *The Magic City: Unemployment in a Working-Class Community.*
            Ithaca: Cornell University Press.
Pearsall, Marion
    1959    *Little Smokey Ridge.* Tuscaloosa: University of Alabama Press.
Perdue, Theda
    1979    *Slavery and the Evolution of Cherokee Society, 1540–1866.* Knox-
            ville: University of Tennessee Press.
Philliber, William W., and Clyde B. McCoy, eds.
    1981    *The Invisible Minority: Urban Appalachians.* Lexington: University
            Press of Kentucky.
Pickard, Jerome
    1981    "Population Changes and Trends in Appalachia." In *Invisible Minor-
            ity: Urban Appalachians,* ed. William W. Philliber and Clyde B. Mc-
            Coy. Lexington: University Press of Kentucky.
Pirenne, Henri
    1937    *Economic and Social History of Medieval Europe.* New York: Har-
            court, Brace and World.
Plakans, Andrejs
    1977    "Identifying Kinfolk beyond the Household." *Journal of Family His-
            tory* 2 : 3–27.
Plattner, Stuart
    1975    *Formal Methods in Economic Anthropology.* Special Publication
            No. 4. Washington, D.C.: American Anthropological Association.
    1986    *Markets and Marketing.* Lanham, Md.: University Press of America.
    1989    "Economic Behavior in Markets." In *Economic Anthropology,* ed.
            Stuart Plattner. Stanford: Stanford University Press.
Plattner, Stuart, ed.
    1985    *Markets and Marketing.* Monographs in Economic Anthropology
            No. 4. Lanham, Md.: University Press of America.
Polanyi, Karl, Conrad Arensberg, and Harry W. Pearson, eds.
    1957    *Trade and Markets in the Early Empires.* Glencoe, Ill.: Free Press.
Precourt, Walter
    1983    "The Image of Appalachian Poverty." In *Appalachia and America:
            Autonomy and Regional Dependence,* ed. Alan Batteau. Lexington:
            University Press of Kentucky.
Pryor, Frederic L.
    1977    *The Origins of the Economy: A Comparative Study of Distribution
            in Primitive and Peasant Economies.* New York: Academic Press.

Raitz, Karl B., and Richard Ulack
  1984    *Appalachia, a Regional Geography: Land, People, and Develop-ment.* Boulder, Col.: Westview Press.
Rubin, Lillian
  1976    *Worlds of Pain: Life in the Working-Class Family.* New York: Basic Books.
Scheffler, Harold W.
  1976    "The 'Meaning' of Kinship in American Culture." In *Meaning in Anthropology,* ed. Keith H. Basso and Henry A. Selby. Albuquerque: University of New Mexico Press.
Schneider, David M.
  1968    *American Kinship: A Cultural Account.* Englewood Cliffs, N.J.: Prentice-Hall.
  1976    "Notes toward a Theory of Culture." In *Meaning in Anthropology,* ed. Keith H. Basso and Henry A. Selby. Albuquerque: University of New Mexico Press.
Schneider, David M., and Raymond T. Smith
  1973    *Class Differences and Sex Roles in American Kinship and Family Structure.* Englewood Cliffs, N.J.: Prentice-Hall.
Schwarzweller, Harry K., and James S. Brown
  1970    "Social Class Origins and Psychological Adjustment of Kentucky Mountain Migrants: A Case Study." In *Behavior in New Environments: Adaptation of Migrant Populations,* ed. Eugene Brody. Beverly Hills: Sage Publications.
Schwarzweller, Harry K., James S. Brown, and J. J. Mangalam, eds.
  1971    *Mountain Families in Transition.* University Park: Pennsylvania State University Press.
Scott, James C.
  1985    *Weapons of the Weak: Everyday Forms of Peasant Resistance.* New Haven: Yale University Press.
Segalen, Martine, and Francoise Zonabend
  1987    "Social Anthropology and the Ethnology of France: The Field of Kinship and the Family." In *Anthropology at Home,* ed. Anthony Jackson. London: Tavistock Publications.
Shapiro, Henry D.
  1978    *Appalachia on Our Mind.* Chapel Hill: University of North Carolina Press.
Siegel, Bernard J., ed.
  1980    *Annual Review of Anthropology.* Vol. 9. Palo Alto: Annual Reviews.
Skinner, G. William
  1964    "Marketing and Social Structure in Rural China." *Journal of Asian Studies* 23:3, 195; 24:363–399.
Smith, Carol
  1974    "Economics of Marketing Systems: Models from Economic Geogra-

phy." In *Annual Review of Anthropology*, vol. 3, ed. Bernard Siegal, Alan R. Beals, and Stephen A. Tyler. Palo Alto: Annual Reviews.

1975    "Examining Stratification Systems through Peasant Marketing Arrangements: An Application of Some Models from Economic Geography." *Man* 10:95–122.

1976a    "Analyzing Regional Social Systems." In vol. 2, *Regional Analysis*, ed. Carol Smith. 2 vols. New York: Academic Press.

1976b    "Markets in Oaxaca, Are They Really Unique?" In *Reviews in Anthropology* 3:387–399.

1977    "How Marketing Systems Affect Economic Opportunity in Agrarian Societies." In *Peasant Livelihood: Studies in Economic Anthropology and Cultural Ecology*, ed. Rhoda Halperin and James Dow. New York: St. Martin's Press.

1983    "Regional Analysis in World-System Perspective: A Critique of Three Structural Theories of Uneven Development." In *Economic Anthropology: Topics and Theories*, ed. Sutti Ortiz. Lanham, Md.: University Press of America.

1985    "Methods for Analysing Periodic Marketplaces as Elements in Regional Trading Systems." In *Research in Economic Anthropology*, vol. 7, ed. Barry L. Isaac. Greenwich, Conn.: JAI Press.

Stack, Carol B.
1974    *All Our Kin.* New York: Harper and Row.

Stein, William W.
1975    "Outside Contact and Cultural Stability in a Peruvian Highland Village." In *A Reader in Culture Change*, vol. 2, ed. Ivan Brady and Barry L. Isaac. Cambridge, Mass.: Schenkman Publishing.

Stephenson, John B.
1968    *Shiloh: A Mountain Community.* Lexington: University Press of Kentucky.

Swetnam, John J.
1978    "Interaction between Urban and Rural Residents in a Guatemalan Marketplace." *Urban Anthropology* 7:137–153.

Taussig, Michael T.
1980    *The Devil and Commodity Fetishism in South America.* Chapel Hill: University of North Carolina Press.

Thompson, Edward P.
1963    *The Making of the English Working Class.* New York: Random House.

Titon, Jeff T.
1988    *Powerhouse for God: Speech, Chant, and Song in an Appalachian Baptist Church.* Austin: University of Texas Press.

Toynbee, Arnold
1947    *A Study of History.* Vol. 2. New York: Oxford University Press.

Trager, Lillian
1985    "From Yams to Beer in a Nigerian City: Expansion and Change in Informal Sector Trade Activity." In *Markets and Marketing*, ed. Stuart Plattner. Monographs in Economic Anthropology No. 4. Lanham, Md.: University Press of America.

Turner, William H.
  1985    *Blacks in Appalachia.* Lexington: University Press of Kentucky.
Van Willigen, John
  1989    *Gettin' Some Age on Me: Social Organization of Older People in a Rural American Community.* Lexington: University Press of Kentucky.
Walls, David
  1978    "Internal Colony or Internal Periphery? A Critique of Current Models and an Alternative Formulation." In *Colonialism in Modern America: The Appalachian Case,* ed. Helen Matthews Lewis, Linda Johnson, and Donald Askins. Boone, N.C.: Appalachian Consortium Press.
Warner, James C.
  1976    "Survey of the Market System in the Nochixtl Valley and the Mixteca Alta." In *Markets in Oaxaca,* ed. Scott Cook and Martin Diskin. Austin: University of Texas Press.
Weinberg, Daniela
  1975    *Peasant Wisdom: Cultural Adaptation in a Swiss Village.* Berkeley and Los Angeles: University of California Press.
Weisner, Thomas S.
  1976    "The Structure of Sociability: Urban Migration and Urban Rural Ties in Kenya." *Urban Anthropology* 5 : 199–224.
Weller, Jack
  1965    *Yesterday's People.* Lexington: University Press of Kentucky.
West, James
  1945    *Plainville, U.S.A.* New York: Columbia University Press.
Whisnant, David E.
  1980    *Modernizing the Mountaineer: People, Power, and Planning in Appalachia.* New York: Burt Franklin.
  1983    *All That Is Native and Fine: The Politics of Culture in an American Region.* Chapel Hill: University of North Carolina Press.
Wilk, Richard R., and Robert M. Netting
  1984    "Households: Changing Forms and Functions." In *Households: Comparative and Historical Studies of the Domestic Group,* ed. Robert M. Netting, Richard R. Wilk, and Eric J. Arnould. Berkeley and Los Angeles: University of California Press.
Williams, Raymond
  1973    *The Country and the City.* New York: Oxford University Press.
Willis, Meredith Sue
  1981    *Higher Ground.* New York: Scribner's.
Wolf, Eric
  1956    "Aspects of Group Relations in a Complex Society: Mexico." *American Anthropologist* 58 : 1065–1078.
  1966    *Peasants.* Englewood Cliffs, N.J.: Prentice-Hall.

# Index

Geographic and personal names have been changed to preserve anonymity. Some names appear as given (first) names only.